THE CARICATURES OF GEORGE CRUIKSHANK

THE CARICATURES OF

GEORGE CRUIKSHANK

JOHN WARDROPER

DAVID R. GODINE

PUBLISHER

BOSTON 1978

First United States edition published 1978 by
DAVID R. GODINE, *Publisher*
306 Dartmouth Street · Boston · Massachusetts 02116
Copyright © John Wardroper 1977
ISBN 0–87923–231–5
LCC No. 77–94112

Made and printed in Great Britain by
Westerham Press, Westerham, Kent
Designed by Peter Guy
Binding design engraved on vinyl by John Lawrence

CONTENTS

All the plates are copperplate etchings, except for
those on pages 84–93, 95–99 and 110–111, which
are wood engravings.

I wish to thank the staffs of the Bodleian Library,
the Guildhall Library, the Victoria and Albert
Museum department of prints and drawings, the
British Library, and above all the British Museum
department of prints and drawings for their
helpful and efficient service over a long period.
I am also grateful to the Camden, Islington, and
Westminster Public Libraries and the Greater
London Record Office for archival information;
and to Ronald Searle, Paris, and David Borowitz,
Chicago, for permission to quote from
Cruikshank manuscripts.

The prints and sketches are reproduced by
courtesy of the trustees of the British Museum and
British Library – except for the following, which
are reproduced by courtesy of the Victoria and
Albert Museum: three sketches in the
introduction ('My dear father', 'Drawn by me'
and the Regent as a pig) and the Balladmonger,
page 111.

INTRODUCTION

George Cruikshank became a Victorian worthy – a spry and quirky one, it is true, yet still very far from the irreverent artist who had come to manhood in the time of the Regent. Although admirers cultivated him with biographies in mind and pressed him to write his life, he revealed little about that young man. He had renounced too much of him. But the work done in his twenties and thirties, his best work, survived unsuppressible and much sought after, to testify to his past vitality, and to remind him of the time when he had first heard himself called a genius.

He found that when printshop browsers came upon the zestful and sometimes scurrilous caricatures he had created an age before, they were inclined to think them the work of an earlier man of the same name. And indeed they were. But whatever he might think of the young Cruikshank, he was never a man to put up with being denied credit for work he had done. At the age of seventy, the one-time caricaturist and devotee of 'late hours, blue ruin and dollies', now aspiring painter in oils and tee-total campaigner, put on show in London a thirteen-foot-wide canvas, *The Triumph of Bacchus*, depicting the evils of drink in a dozen easy lessons. And round the exhibition hall he also put on display, from the vast hoard of his portfolios, more than a thousand drawings, etchings and engravings, some of them dating from his eighth year: to prove, as he said in the catalogue, 'that I am not my own grandfather'.

It was a self-censored selection. Cruikshank could not of course be expected to offend the proprieties of 1863 (and of his temperance associates) by exhibiting any Regency lewdness; but the selectiveness went much further than that. Although George IV had been dead for a third of a century, Cruikshank showed none of his rumbustious images of that gross Adonis and his outsize mistresses, nor any of the caricatures he had done in that reign on the radical side. This editing of his past was noticed. The *Art Journal* recalled in particular a famous series of anti-establishment woodcuts done by Cruikshank in 1820, and said, 'It will scarcely be credited that not one of these famous designs appears'. He had 'ignored the very existence of works that all admire and covet' and had 'done himself an injustice in his own gallery'.[1] He had evidently gone further than some Victorians thought necessary in adjusting the evidence of his former less decorous self. It was a timid celebration by the man who had had the good fortune to be born soon enough to flourish as the last great master caricaturist of the Georgian era.

George Cruikshank was a child of the eighteenth century and of London. He was born in Duke Street (now Coptic Street), Bloomsbury, on 27 September 1792.[2] And he was the child of an artist. His father, Isaac

Cruikshank, son of a Scottish customs officer, had been working in London as a caricaturist, illustrator and engraver since migrating from Edinburgh, probably in 1784, when he was twenty-one. Four years later he found a bride among London's large community of Scots: Mary MacNaughton, a girl of eighteen from Perth. They were married on 14 August 1788 at St Anne's Church, Soho. When their first child, Isaac Robert, was born 13 months later, they were in lodgings in St Martin's Court, Westminster; but in 1792 Isaac and Mary were able to take a whole house (at twenty-eight pounds a year plus rates, or more than many labourers earned in a year) in Bloomsbury, a few minutes' walk from green fields.

It was still the eighteenth century, but a new age was beginning. The king and queen of France were prisoners, and five days before George was born, the leaders of the revolution had proclaimed a republic. In London, another royal person, George Prince of Wales, who was to be a gift to Isaac and George and every caricaturist for years to come, was writing to his mother in great agitation about agents who were going round the alehouses 'propagating those *damnable doctrines* of the *hell-begotten Jacobines*'.[3] He had personal reasons for fearing those doctrines, for his witless extravagance had got him over £400,000 in debt and his creditors were threatening to send the bailiffs into Carlton House, his ostentatious private palace.[4]

The choice of the name George for the baby might seem to imply some reverence for George III and his family, but Isaac Cruikshank's caricatures hardly support this. (The choice was perhaps inspired rather by the fact that the baptism was at St George's, Bloomsbury.) A few months earlier, Isaac published, for example, a caricature that is ostensibly about an anti-slavery campaigners' boycott of West Indies sugar, but which really says something more piquant. The king, queen and two of the princesses are round a tea-table, and twenty-two-year-old Princess Elizabeth is saying, 'Indeed papa, I can't leave off a good thing so soon. I am sure of late I have been very moderate, but I must have a bit now and then.' This alludes to Elizabeth's pregnancies of the 1780s. George III replies, 'Poo poo poo, leave it off at once. You know I have never drank any since I was married, Lizzie' – that is, not had any illicit attachments. The other princess, probably Sophia, who also found ways to make up for the parents' failure to find the girls husbands, says, 'For my *part* I'd rather want altogether than have a small *piece*.'[5]

Nor was Isaac by any means a steady loyalist over greater questions. When George was a fortnight old, and the French had routed an army led by the Duke of Brunswick, George III's brother-in-law, Isaac pictured the Germans defecating in terror as they fled from brave sans-culottes. Later, within a month of Louis XVI's execution, Isaac depicted France as a comely woman lashing the monarchs of Europe as 'religious bigots, perverters of public justice, oppressors of the people' and so forth. They ride on an ass, which excretes into the mouth of a prostrate Louis. At the very same period, however, Isaac savagely attacked Thomas Paine and the scientist-reformer Joseph Priestley as sinister 'friends of the people' equipped with pistols, daggers, swords and barrels of gun-powder, and with books and papers labelled 'assassination – massacres – treasons – downfall of royalty – plunder – the Rights of Man'. The English were still in two minds about the revolution (it might be all right for the backward French). The work of Isaac Cruikshank neatly demonstrates what was true of many caricaturists: they made use of passing events in a detached and perhaps cynical way; but as they had always to aim at winning a wide response, everything they did had to look to a body of opinion. It is for this reason that caricatures are one of the most sensitive, as well as much the liveliest, guides to the many-sided truth of past times.

Isaac Cruikshank had higher ambitions as well. When still living in St Martin's Court he had had two paintings accepted by the Royal Academy (then at Somerset House in the Strand), *Return to Lochaber* and *Visit to the Cottage*; and in 1792 he showed a third, *The Distresses and Triumphs of Virtue*.[6] All sound like sentimental narrative pictures. They were, however, the last he exhibited. He did give art lessons, though, and one pupil, George Dawe, became an RA. Perhaps Dawe shared lessons with the Cruikshank boys: a sheet of sketches survives on which a boyish hand has written, 'George Dawe is a villin'.[7] The villin grew to have a reputation for unamiable self-advancement, and was said to have earned £100,000 painting portraits of European royalty.

With a growing family, Isaac was perhaps under pressure to win a dependable income from less esteemed crafts than academy painting. He would accept most jobs: illustrations for nursery rhymes and children's stories; frontispieces for jestbooks and songbooks; puffs for lottery promoters; and sometimes more serious commissions, such as a share in the illustrating of a many-volume *General Zoology* which began appearing in 1800. For this he worked in the British Museum while little George and Robert played in the vast garden behind, where London University's graceless Senate House now stands. All these jobs were supplementary: his main activity over more than twenty years was the creation of comic and satirical caricature prints.

In the years following George's birth the family made further moves, until by 1808 it was established in a large house, of basement and four floors, in Dorset Street (now Dorset Rise): a strategic place for Isaac's freelance craft, a minute's walk south of Fleet Street, an artery of the printing and publishing trade. Scores of firms, with shops on the street-front and usually with their own presses behind, were in lively com-petition in and near Fleet Street, eastwards round St Paul's and beyond, and westwards along the Strand and as far as fashionable St James's.

And Isaac was doing well, in book illustration as well as caricaturing. His wife Mary, a forceful, managing woman, is said to have prided herself on having put aside the great sum of £1,000 in those years.[8]

For an artist who gave up academic ambitions (as James Gillray had done some years earlier), a steady income from caricaturing was not the only consolation. A caricaturist was freed from wooing the uncertain favour of well-to-do patrons in the picture-buying world. If one of his caricatures in the window of a London printshop or a stationer any-where in the kingdom stirred an impulse of delight that made a man spend a shilling or two, he had found a patron. He was far more inde-pendent than cartoonists of a later age: he did not work for a newspaper, with a policy and a family readership to consider, and only rarely for magazines. Each separate work he created could thus be untrammelled by cant of politics or good taste, shaped only by the artist's inspiration and the need to appeal to the contemporary eye. He was valued in all ranks of society. People too poor to buy a single print could still stand laughing (and extending their political education) in the crowds which since Hogarth's day had been notorious for blocking the pavement in front of the printshops' crowded panes. Gentlemen and noble lords collected caricatures by the hundred in portfolios and bound volumes. Colonel Grantley Berkeley of Berkeley Castle, born 1800, says in his memoirs, 'I remember well the unfailing resource for the entertainment of guests in large country houses of the book of caricatures. Those un-fortunates who cannot be got to talk . . . become social over a portfolio of ludicrous scenes . . . and ancient tabbies have been found to grow quite amiable . . . as the more equivocal prints were turned over. It was the custom before my day, and in my youth, to get all the novelties of this kind from London as regularly as the fashionable novel or the last new ballad.'[9] For Isaac Cruikshank as for Gillray, the direction he took was not a defeat.

And it was the shaping of his son George. Long afterwards he said, 'I was cradled in caricature.'[10] He made several drawings of his remembered self, a plump-faced boy, leaning on the work-table of 'my dear father', watching him drawing and etching. Sometimes his father would be creating ink-and-watercolour designs from which other engravers would etch a plate. More often he would see his father both making his design and etching it on a copperplate (usually measuring about nine inches by fourteen), ready for a printseller's press. The man for whom Isaac mainly made his plates was S. W. Fores, who had the most prolific caricature shop of the time – first at No. 3 Piccadilly (a site long since overwhelmed by Piccadilly Circus) and then at No. 50. The subjects were most often political; some examples have already been described. Isaac's carica-tures for Fores were in direct competition with Gillray's work at Hannah Humphrey's shop in Bond Street and later in St James's Street, and some-times they attained an almost Gillrayesque savagery.

At Isaac's next most important outlet, the firm of Laurie & Whittle at 53 Fleet Street, everything was aimed at people looking for a jovial laugh or an equivocal giggle. It was here that Isaac took his pen-and-water-

'My dear Father & myself': drawn by George Cruikshank many years later

colour drawings (of which 112 survive in a bound volume at the Huntington Collection in California).[11] They were an early equivalent of cartoon jokes, but were often much more ribald than was later thought proper for newspapers and magazines. Frequent subjects were the endless war of the sexes (women often triumphing), ridiculous fashions, comic mishaps, and stock social targets such as grasping lawyers and bloated parsons. Sometimes the etching was an illustration to a comic song, with the words beneath; sometimes a faithful old jest in visual form – of the wench whose baby was only a little one, or of the wife who, when told by her husband that only one man in their street was not a cuckold, was puzzled to know which husband it could be (these both go back to the seventeenth century). Laurie & Whittle made a virtue of its unfraught themes in its catalogue of 1795, when dear bread and radical ideas were agitating the country. It offers 'the greatest variety of whimsical, satirical and burlesque subjects (but not political) . . . well calculated for the shop windows of country booksellers and stationers, etc.'[12] These prints, known as drolls, were smaller than the general run of caricatures, and at sixpence plain, one shilling coloured they were about half the price. Even so, they were not for poor men: a farm labourer might need a day's wage to buy a coloured one. He had to be content to study them in shop windows, or stuck on the wall in the alehouse bar, next to broadside ballads and government-subsidized verses and dialogues warning in artful homely style against the perilous ideas of Tom Paine.

Both the drolls and the more sophisticated caricatures nourished almost everything that is lasting in George Cruikshank's work. The drolls taught him how to raise laughter by simple means, as the best jokes do, by building on the awkwardness and imperfection of life, or by mirroring man's unthinking follies. In the work for Fores he learned that a caricaturist had more purposes than to amuse. He might be inspired by a Commons debate as well as by tavern gossip, and could comment on the fall of a kingdom as boldly as on the fall of a neckline. The satirical prints conveyed news, they joined in the political fight, they taught people not to view their superiors with excessive reverence. They paraded the likenesses of public figures more tellingly than suave official portraits ever do (and this in itself gives them lasting value). They were almost above the law: a fear of compounding the ridicule had long made victims refrain from taking action against statements which if printed in the newspapers might easily have brought convictions for libel. Royal persons were not above having newspapers brought into court, but the Prince of Wales and his brothers never ventured to act against the grossest suggestions in caricatures. An example, and by no means an extreme one, is a caricature that Isaac Cruikshank did in 1795 when the Prince of Wales, by consenting to marry, had got parliament to settle his debts, by then more than £600,000. It shows him at a 'meeting of creditors' – an array of bawds displaying overdue bills for all sorts of brothel specialities: 'Wheelbarrow £100, sky rocket £100, rods £10, à la Rome £200, a first slice of a nice titbit only 12 years and 6 hours £1000 . . .'[13]

What line was taken on such things by Mary Cruikshank, who by several accounts was a sternminded member of the Church of Scotland? Perhaps her interest in money outweighed her piety; and besides, caricatures on wastrel princes or dissolute lords could be seen as smiting the wickedness of the mighty.

One influence on the caricatures that George watched his father making was Thomas Rowlandson. Isaac is certain to have known Rowlandson well, for both men etched plates from the comic designs of a convivial artist named George Moutard Woodward (before Woodward died in a Bow Street tavern in 1809, young George also etched for him). But the greatest single influence, first on the father and then on George, was James Gillray, who in the 1790s and early 1800s was at the height of his power, known throughout the kingdom, famous and imitated even on the continent. Isaac even adopted a Gillrayesque phrasing in his caricature titles, such as 'A Panic on Both Sides', or 'Great Men in the Horrors !!'; and he was not above plagiarizing for Fores from a new Gillray on sale at Hannah Humphrey's. George was later to do Gillray the honour of creating variations on Gillray themes and working in his manner. In his prime, George was quoted as saying of Gillray's work: 'He that did these things was a great man, sir – a very great man, sir.'[14]

Before the new century began, George was learning the techniques of the pencil, pen and watercolour brush, and then the etching needle.

'When I was a mere boy,' he wrote seventy years later, 'my dear father kindly allowed me to *play* at *etching* on some of his copperplates – little bits of shadow, or little figures in the background – and to assist him a *little* as I grew older, and he used to assist *me* in putting in hands and faces.'[15] The earliest prints George did for money were suitably innocent things: uncoloured comic or patriotic figures for a halfpenny; children's lottery prints bearing rows of rough pictures of boats, buildings or animals (one of these in his 1863 exhibition was described as 'the first design he was employed to do, and paid for'); or topical subjects such as, in 1805, Nelson's ornate funeral carriage. Before he progressed to caricatures, he was following his father in etching frontispieces for songbooks, dreambooks and jestbooks, and illustrating chapbooks of the Mother Goose type.

His lessons in his father's studio were complemented by the lessons he could absorb in the streets. His neighbourhood provided a medley of the high, middling and low: gentlemen, merchants, master craftsmen, artisans of a dozen trades, and rough riverside labourers down at the foot of his street. In his earliest surviving sketches may be seen evidence of his eye for action, gesture and dramatic suggestiveness: the contrasting antics of spectators lining the route of a royal procession, for example, or the surly arrogance of a gentleman dropping coins into the hat of an anxious beggar. Every satirical artist needs a theatrical eye. 'My picture was my stage,' said Hogarth, 'and men and women my actors who were by means of certain actions and expressions to exhibit a dumbshow.'[16] And it was the theatre, indeed, that was George Cruikshank's first ambition, after he had been talked out of a boyhood idea of being a sailor. All his life he loved play-acting. A sketch survives of himself as a little boy, his face framed in fur, his eyes staring, his teeth bared – with this note: 'George Cruikshank when a boy used to put his mothers Fur Tippet over his head like the above and make frightful faces for *fun*.'[17] In his teens he performed in juvenile theatre companies – a lively nursery for actors at that time. The event that came to decide his career was the death of his father.

The date of Isaac Cruikshank's death has hitherto been left uncertain: either 1810 or 1811. The vagueness is unnecessary. The records of his parish church, St Bride's, which stands a few yards from Dorset Rise, show that he was buried on 16 April 1811, aged forty-eight. The cause of death (as for many others at the time) is given as 'decline', which often meant tuberculosis, but does not disprove later statements that drinking killed him. Certainly he was a drinker, and in a hard-drinking age. Perhaps the less genial nature of his wife helped to drive him to the tavern; one account has it that whenever she invited the Church of Scotland minister to the house (and one holder of the post was James Steven, founder of the London Missionary Society), Isaac would slip away across Fleet Street to the Ben Jonson in Shoe Lane.[18] He was a member of a club of press and theatre men, The Brilliants,[19] who met at The Swan, Chandos Street, Charing Cross, after curtain-fall, and sat drinking, reciting and singing until 4 or 5 a.m. The club chairman for

'Drawn by me when a little boy': George's note on a sketch

[10]

many years was James Laurie of Laurie & Whittle; and in January 1801 Isaac did two prints for him, one showing members drunkenly fighting, and the other, all in more or less comatose states, with only the chairman on his feet and singing. In the same month a print by the tavern-loving Thomas Rowlandson, 'The Brilliants', shows them in action, mostly jovial, but three of them vomiting; and on the wall are the following 'rules to be observed in this society':

1 Each member shall fill a half pint bumper to the first toast. 2 After twenty-four bumper toasts are gone round, every [member] may fill as he pleases. 3 Any member refusing to comply with the above regulations to be fined a bumper of salt and water.

Probably Rowlandson exaggerates; perhaps the drink was a dilute punch; but the salt water must have served to prolong some of their lives.

When Isaac Cruikshank died, George was eighteen-and-a-half. His brother Robert had already set himself up as a portrait painter at 15 Dean Street, Soho. George found himself in the role of breadwinner for his mother and a four-year-old sister. It was at this point, however, that he made an attempt to avoid succeeding to his father. 'The applause with which he was received both in comic and serious parts at the various juvenile theatres where he appeared led him to anticipate a very successful career as an actor,' says a biographical work issued in 1834 by one of his publishers. 'To become, indeed, a great actor was his ambition, but the preliminary steps of a stroller's life were not consonant to his feelings.'[20] It would have to be the London theatre or nothing. His recollection of what happened is given in an autobiographical sketch he wrote at the age of sixty-seven: 'He thought of becoming an assistant scene painter at one of the London theatres and then working his way on the stage as an actor, having evinced considerable dramatic ability – amongst his youthful associates – both in comedy & tragedy – and always performing the part of scene painter to these juvenile companies. In order to get a proper and respectable introduction – he applied to a friend of his late father – Mr James Whittle – of the firm of Whittle & Laurie – publisher – to introduce him to Mr Raymond – the then manager of Drury Lane Theatre. Mr Whittle told him to paint a scene upon a piece of mill board to show to Mr Raymond – this was imposing an unexpected task – for which Master George had neither the inclination nor the spare time to execute he being then fully occupied in making drawings on wood for children's books – and so this little scene was never painted – and so our artist neither became a scene painter nor an actor.'[21]

In fact he was doing much more than children's woodblocks by this time. He was achieving his first mature caricatures; and that no doubt helped to save him from having to swallow his pride and produce the sample for Drury Lane. His pride is probably the clue to another incident a little earlier. According to William Clarke, a journalist who knew him well, George wished to study at the Royal Academy, as his brother had done. He took a sample of his work – a drawing of an antique figure – along the Strand to show to Henry Fuseli, the academy's sharp-tongued Keeper and professor of painting. 'Well, you may go in, but you must fight for a seat,' Fuseli said. Clarke's account goes on: 'The students were so numerous that he could not approach near enough even to see the outlines of the principal figures – his powers of vision being, at that time, particularly weak.' Was this temporary shortsightedness a later invention of George's? He did not fight for a seat a second time, and the nearest he came to academy training, until many years later, was to attend one course of lectures.

'He determined on studying life itself,' says Clarke's article. 'His gallery was the tap-room of a low public house . . . towards the Thames' frequented by 'Irish coal-whippers, Billingsgate Bellonas [fish-market women], Black Sals [scavengers], Dusty Bobs [dustmen], etc., whose frolics and features he was accustomed to study, night after night, through a friendly hole in the shutter which he had picked out for the purpose with his graver. Hence his matchless delineations of low life . . . His fights are nothing like "effusions of fancy"; they do not resemble a scene that *might* be, but one . . . that has been.'[22] It is revealing to find that he became touchy about this low public house, or at least about any inference that he had descended so low as to have been 'the companion of dustmen, hodmen, coal-heavers and scavengers'. In the first number of his own periodical, *George Cruikshank's Omnibus*, in 1842, he is moved to write at length about the place. It was The Lion in the Wood in Wilderness Lane (now Hutton Street), a turning off Dorset Street, then almost beside the unembanked Thames. 'It was frequented by coal-heavers only,' he says, raising it slightly in the social world. Then follows a striking expression of his remembered response to the vitality of a gathering of humble people. He says that one night his attention was especially attracted by the sound of a fiddle, and when he looked through the window into the crowded tap-room he noticed over the chimney-piece a bust of Shakespeare with a pipe stuck in its mouth. 'It was a palpable meeting of the Sublime and the Ridiculous; the world of Intellect and Poetry seemed thrown open to the meanest capacity; extremes had met; the highest and the lowest had united in harmonious fellowship; . . . and feeling that even he might have well wished to be there the pleased spectator of that lower world, it was impossible not to recognise the fitness of the pipe . . . What a picture of life was there! . . . It was *all* life. In simpler words, I saw, on approaching the window and peeping between the short red curtains, a swarm of jolly coal-heavers! Coal-heavers all – save a few of the fairer and softer sex – the wives of some of them – all enjoying the hour with an intensity not to be disputed, and in a manner singularly characteristic of the tastes and propensities of aristocratic and fashionable society; that is to say, they were "dancing and taking refreshments" . . . This incident . . . led me to study the characters of that particular class of society; and laid the foundation of scenes afterwards published.'[23] In his caricatures and other work there is evidence that he was both attracted and perturbed (like Dickens) by the lower orders. He certainly did not study them only by peeping between the curtains; as a youth and young man he spent more time in fellowship with them than he wished to say at the age of fifty.

Detail from 'Interior View of the House of God', 1811, with self-portrait of George (see below)

When George Cruikshank opted for caricature in 1811, the trade had lost two leading artists: some months before his father's death, James Gillray had lapsed into madness. The most prolific surviving caricaturists were Rowlandson, who was doing little political work, and a man now almost forgotten, Charles Williams. And just at this time a new scene was opening, a fruitful one for the trade. George III's mind had withdrawn from the world (some historians quibble strangely over the word 'mad'), and the Prince of Wales, on being declared Regent, had confounded his old friends the Whigs by keeping the Tories in power. Suddenly the man who had hitherto been little more than outrageous, ridiculous, infuriating, became a prime political target. Whig wits who had kept silent, in the hope of power, now planted squibs in the Whig newspapers, thought up lampoons, and fed ideas to the caricaturists. Then in 1812 a new scene opened on the continent too. Napoleon marched to Moscow, and returned; and an end to the long wars at last seemed possible. It was a good time to be an artist of nineteen and flowing with ideas.

We know how the young man looked then, how he dressed his hair, what he wore – for he put himself in one corner of a large caricature, 'Interior View of the House of God', just after his nineteenth birthday. He is the stylish fellow, second from the left, wearing frilly shirt, light-coloured breeches and a tailcoat, with pencil and sketchbook in one hand and a gentlemanly high hat in the other. He is talking to William Naunton Jones, publisher of *The Scourge*, a satirical magazine in which the caricature appeared in November 1811. Immediately behind George is a man with whom he was to collaborate within a few years on some famous pamphlets: the radical publisher William Hone. The man listening to Hone is George's brother.

Here is George Cruikshank 'studying life itself', and of course pointing up the grotesqueness of what he saw. The caricature was an attack on a dubious religious meeting-house run by a man named Elias Carpenter (a former partner of the fraudulent Joanna Southcote), who sold the credulous cheap tickets to salvation. The place was alleged to be a scene of 'libidinous fervour'. *The Scourge* sounds shocked: 'To the orgies of this place, the young, the innocent, the stripling and the virgin are indiscriminately admitted; they witness scenes that might shock the feelings of the atheist and raise a blush on the cheek of prostitution . . . Mr ———— is authorized by the Angel Gabriel to keep a wife and have at the same time as many concubines as he pleases.' [24] (The dash is a guard against a libel suit.) Cruikshank shows an unsavoury congregation. In the row above him, the fat woman with patched face is a bawd. A lecher is wooing a girl with the aid of Cleland's *Fanny Hill*. The girl's coy sidelong curiosity is nicely caught; the old woman behind is less coy. Over to the right, the label beneath the praying man reads, 'Capt Morris's Hymns – Hymn 1st Great Plenipo' – meaning 'The Plenipotentiary', one of the best-known bawdy songs of the time, often sung in the Prince of Wales's circle.

So here is a young man who is no innocent. He already has the knowingness his job requires. Through his associations with the publishing trade and his enthusiasm for the theatre he is likely by this time to have been involved already in late-night free-and-easy merriment (he succeeded his father as a member of The Brilliants). In the streets he would see temptations enough; and the lobbies of the theatres, both in the West End and the suburbs, were notoriously the haunts of the more presentable prostitutes. The magazine *Town Talk* says in November 1811: 'Those houses which are opened for the purpose of pantomimic shows and minor representations are the fertile hotbeds of depravity, the well-stored warehouses for the wholesale supply of the Cyprian market.' It attacks in particular a theatre George was frequenting then, Robert Elliston's Surrey Theatre, as a School for Vice where 'equivocal elegantes . . . spread their snares for higher game than apprentices and shopmen' and 'delight in *semi-nudity*'. [25]

Was the Regency a particularly rakish time? It seemed so to some. 'Many years have not elapsed since obscenity was regarded as disgraceful,' says *The Scourge* two months later. 'But the philosophers of our times are of opinion that vice becomes less dangerous the better it is known.' It complains that 'the most indecorous prints and indelicate advertisements are daily exhibited . . . which a few years ago would have subjected their exhibitors to a dungeon or the pillory'. But the best example it can give is this: 'The windows of the petty book shops have been for some time decorated with a print of Dick v Dick, on a delicate question of sexual potency' – so it seems to be partly a case of one publisher deploring its spicier competitors. [26] *The Scourge* was certainly capable of lashing in several directions. A few months earlier it satirized the Society for the Suppression of Vice, and on two reasonable grounds: the society pursued the humble but spared noble and royal sinners; and

its activists were prurient in their vice-hunting. In a parody Report of the Society for the Persecution of the Poor, it said: '. . . Every unmarried female above the age of fourteen detected in assisting a male child to perform the urinary office should be committed to the county gaol . . . The pairing of canary birds in apartments to which females have access should be strongly prohibited . . . and every object that bears a phallic outline should be banished from our dwellings and razed from our streets . . . The society have engaged a numerous train of active and intelligent informers: men who can detect a couple of fleas in *actu coitus*, and who are well acquainted with all the varieties of obscenity.' [27]

In the eyes of censorious people, one proof of moral decline could be seen in the revealing dress of fashionable women. Trade with the east had made diaphanous materials plentiful; and liberating notions of the 1790s had encouraged women to throw off their stays and flaunt their breasts. At Sadler's Wells, Joey Grimaldi dressed up as The Fashionable Lady, in muslin and 'my dashing Egyptian shawl', and sang:

> You'll own that my style's pretty high.
>   So transparent my dress, you can see thro' it;
> The ladies all wear such, and cry,
>   'O curse you, no, don't look at me thro' it.'
> I wonder what ladies can mean
>   Who in dress so transparent their bodies tie.
> I blush like a maid of fifteen –
>   To see 'em, it quite shocks my modesty.
>   *Ri fol-lol de-rol . . .*[28]

The free-and-easy ladies were naturally associated with criticism of the Regent and his friends, whose style was so different from that of old Farmer George. Under the heading Royal Nudity, the influence of the Regent's court was lamented by yet another satirical journal, *The Busy Body*: 'We all know pretty well what is the private disposition and what are the pursuits of the Prince Regent; they have naturally communicated their influence throughout the sphere in which he moves, and the consequence is that the appearance of a [royal] drawing-room is very like the aspect of the saloons at the two theatres just at the close of the performances.'[29] That is, the ladies looked like courtesans.

For young George Cruikshank, sketchbook in hand, there were subjects in plenty, and soon he was selling his caricature ideas to twenty printsellers. The appetite for caricatures continued to be enormous. There was nothing else (except the theatre, and it was politically neutered) to translate the newspapers' unillustrated, almost unheadlined words into visual drama. The sole innovation in periodical publishing was the insertion of a large coloured folding caricature, instead of a small plain one, in each issue of *The Scourge* and its competitors. For the caricaturists, this was an extension of the market and a source of extra publicity; and the magazines were a channel for ideas. They welcomed anonymous contributions from readers. After having used one lampoon and sketch that inspired a Cruikshank caricature on the

Regent, *The Scourge* says in its April 1812 issue: 'To our Piccadilly correspondent . . . we labour under particular obligations; and beg leave to suggest the Coronation of the Empress as a fit sequel to the other. The individual pictures should be distinct.' Cruikshank did this sequel in due course.

The Regent was a great buyer of caricatures – when they were not about him. Bills preserved at Windsor show that as prince regent and

Sketches by George of the Regent as a pig ready for the butcher's axe. He seems not to have published any such caricature: perhaps he feared he might be charged with sedition

king, from 1782 until his death in 1830, he bought thousands. He had standing accounts with several printsellers; and in an eighteen-month period of 1806–07, for example, he bought 121 caricatures from Hannah Humphrey alone.[30] A great many of these, incidentally, were against the Whigs whose friend he then ostensibly was. He was glad to laugh at others. What he could never tolerate was a caricature or a lampoon that ridiculed his own extravagance, folly, irresponsibility, grossness and cowardice.

Cruikshank, busy ridiculing the Regent as exuberantly as anyone, seems to have been motivated primarily, like nearly all caricaturists, by his delight in a good paying subject. He was willing to work for men of all opinions – the radical John Fairburn and William Hone, the independent or whiggish *Scourge, Town Talk* and *Meteor,* the middle-of-the-road S. W. Fores and Thomas Tegg, the increasingly conservative Hannah Humphrey and the Tory-supported *Satirist.* However, in these early years his radical and whiggish work seems to reflect more personal feeling; and when he did eight successive plates for *The Satirist*

(1813–14) he managed to avoid subjects that involved him in its aggressive anti-Whig, pro-Regent line (he had poor declining Boney for a ready alternative). Neither in those days nor later did he entirely merit the description used by J. G. Lockhart in *Blackwood's Magazine* in 1823: 'A free-handed comical young fellow, who will do anything he is paid for.'[31] He would do *almost* anything. From the start his industry was enormous; and when he was only twenty he felt secure enough in his freelance role to risk irritating three of his employers. In a large frontispiece in the first number of *The Meteor,* he showed the newcomer routing *The Scourge, Town Talk* and *Satirist,* although he was still working for them. *The Meteor* particularly attacked *The Satirist* and its editor, George Manners, who within a few years was to be rewarded for his Tory propaganda with a consul's job in Boston. 'The new class of modern satirists founded by Manners shall meet their merited exposure,' says *The Meteor.* 'We *know* them, their iniquities, their *fees,* and their *paymasters.*'[32]

By 1813, his caricature output had surpassed that of his strongest rivals, Rowlandson and Williams, if the numbers that survive in the British Museum's vast collection are an accurate guide. His brother had returned to Dorset Street in 1812, and soon George was converting the portrait artist into a caricaturist. According to William Clarke, the brothers soon put up their charges. 'The market price of large caricatures, drawn and etched, copper included, had usually been twenty-five or thirty shillings; Isaac Robert insisted on their being quoted in future at three guineas [sixty-three shillings]. What could the poor publishers do?' Clarke adds sardonically. 'It is said their average profits on each plate were reduced, by the gross overcharge, from fifty guineas to fifty pounds seventeen shillings, or thereabouts. This was too bad, considering the unfortunate publishers drank wine, and had their gigs to keep.'[33]

The brothers' studio 'was a strange workroom, decorated with the most incongruous ornaments', says Blanchard Jerrold in his biography of 1882. 'An undergraduate's cap . . . upon a human skull with a pipe between the teeth, a sou'wester from Margate, boxing gloves, foils, masks, and weapons of all kinds, proclaimed the wild tastes of the two artists, who generally invited their guests to a bout with the gloves.'[34] There is nothing very strange about these things, however; nor about the brothers' fondness for boxing and fencing – sports commonly practised by young men of high rank. The Cruikshanks knew the boxer John Jackson, Byron's trainer and friend, and perhaps it was sparring with Jackson that gave George his permanently bent nose. George kept a sketch by Robert of 'Rogers, a black man & fencing master & who taught my brother Robert & me to fence – & who was a total abstainer';[35] and another sketch of himself in boxer's pose, bare to the waist, exhibiting a muscular torso and arm. 'He is described at this early time,' says Jerrold, 'as gifted with extraordinary animal spirits, and filled with a reckless spirit of adventure.' The elder brother had many friends in the sporting world, and no doubt led George into even more late nights. 'The exploits of the wild brothers . . . were severely condemned by their strict mother.'[36] If drink it was that caused her husband's early death, she had reason to feel anxious. The conflicts in George that can already be glimpsed at this time – between high ambition and frivolity, moral purpose and fragmented irreverence – may partly have had their source in the confusing influences of the stern, hardheaded mother and the easy-going father who had taken refuge in taverns.

When one tries to assess the developing mind of this steely-eyed, jesting, opinionated, frolicsome, combative roysterer, a minor streak of consistency can be found in his uncomplex John Bullism. Britain had been at war from his infancy; in the war's closing years he trained as a London volunteer with the Loyal North Britons (that is, Scots); from boy-hood he had a special passion for the navy. Some men had mixed feelings about Napoleon, but not George Cruikshank. 'I can scarcely remember the time when I did not take some patriotic pleasure in persecuting the great enemy of England.' he wrote thirty years later in his *Omnibus*. 'Had he been less than that, I should have felt some compunction for my cruelties . . . insulting, degrading and deriding him everywhere, and putting him to several humiliating deaths.'[37] Frenchmen in general, and other foreigners, were inferior and often ridiculous: on this and on most other points he thought with the majority.

He must have found it hard, then, to go very far with the view of his friend William Hone that Waterloo was a tragedy – a view shared by William Hazlitt and some other unconforming men who could not forget their high hopes of the 1790s or who feared a return to the old absolutism. On one thing, however, he seems to have agreed with Hone passionately: his hatred of the Holy Alliance, and especially of the restored Spanish Inquisition. Perhaps memories of his Church of Scotland teaching gave him a firm belief on this point when he was inclined to be two-sided on so much else (and of course John Bull was no friend of the Pope). At any rate, the fervent complexity of several large caricatures he did on the subject for Hone and others suggests strong involvement; and so does the fact that in 1823, when he had almost ceased to touch on politics, Louis XVIII's campaign to restore the tottering absolutist regime in Spain roused him to a flurry of activity.

Cruikshank's long friendship with Hone throws some light on the artist's mind. Hone was born in 1780, and vividly remembered a day in July 1789 when an excited boy told him in the street, 'There's a revolution in France.'[38] At the age of sixteen he joined the London Correspond-ing Society, the first reform movement organized not by gentlemen but by artisans and humbler men disillusioned with the Whigs' divided and devious policies. In 1801 Hone set up a press in association with a printer named Kidd Wake,[39] who had just finished serving five years in jail merely for shouting 'No George, no war' during a demonstration against George III.

By 1811, when Cruikshank pictured Hone as one of his friends, the older man must have been, or at least hoping to be, one of his mentors in politics. They could easily agree in deriding the Regent; but the association went deeper than that. When in 1817 Hone was put on trial on hypocritical charges of blasphemous libel for publishing satires on the

government in the form of parodies of the Church of England liturgy, Cruikshank helped with his defence by providing examples of earlier parodies – including some by Gillray – that had never been prosecuted because, as Hone said in court, they were 'on the right side'. Hone per-suaded three successive juries to acquit him, having spoken in his own defence, with piles of books and caricatures in front of him, for a total of twenty-one hours. One man pleased at the news was S. W. Fores, who

Sketch made by George in the 1860s of himself and William Hone, probably representing the time when Hone was preparing for his trial in 1817

wrote, 'I heartily rejoice in your defeat of the giant oppression.'[40] (Wordsworth, however, thought it was 'enough to make one out of love with English juries'.)

Two years later came a joint work of Hone and Cruikshank that was remarkable in several ways, and not least because it put Cruikshank's work into the hands of nearly 100,000 buyers (so that, in those days of organized sharing, it was seen, perhaps, by a million people). This was *The Political House That Jack Built*, written by Hone in the aftermath of the Peterloo outrage. As Hone remembered it years later, the idea 'flashed across my mind' when his four-year-old daughter was sitting on his knee looking at her *House That Jack Built*. This and other illustrated nursery rhymes had inspired parodies before. Hone's innovation was to present the parody not as a single etched print, limited in wordage and capable of a run of a few thousand only, but as a twenty-four-page letter-press pamphlet with a dozen integral illustrations. The secret lay in doing the engravings in boxwood, a technique that Thomas Bewick and his school had brought to perfection in that generation. In a wood en-graving, the image is printed from what stands up from the surface, just as words are from typefaces, so the two can be printed simultaneously from the same press, cheaply and rapidly, and in scores of thousands. Hone's illustrated pamphlet, printed on his own press at 45 Ludgate Hill, went for only a shilling – no more than one full-size uncoloured caricature.

Hone's memory of the creating of *The Political House That Jack Built* was that he sat up all night writing the verses, and then: 'In the morning, I sent for Cruikshank, read it to him, and put myself into the attitudes of the figures I wanted drawn. Some of the characters Cruikshank had never seen; but I gave him the likeness as well as the attitude.'[41] Hone, like Cruikshank, was a lover of the theatre; but it is likely that Cruikshank did his share of the attitude-casting for this and for five other pamphlets he illustrated for Hone in the next eighteen months. Another picture of them at work is given in the memoirs of a publisher, Charles Knight, quoting a friend who was present.

'Three friends . . . are snugly ensconced in a private room of a well-accustomed tavern. Hone produces his scheme for The House That Jack Built. He reads some of his doggerel lines. The author wants a design for an idea that is clear enough in words, but is beyond the range of pictorial representation. The artist pooh-poohs. The bland publisher is pertinacious, but not dictatorial. My friend, Alfred Fry, the most earnest, straightforward and argumentative of men . . . cannot vanquish or convince George Cruikshank. "Wait a minute," says the artist. The wine – perhaps the grog – is on the table. He dips his finger in his glass. He rapidly traces wet lines on the mahogany. A single figure starts into life. Two or three smaller figures come out around the first head and trunk – a likeness in its grotesqueness. The publisher cries "Hoorah." . . . A pen-and-ink sketch is completed on the spot. The bottle circulates briskly or the rummers are replenished. Politics are the theme, whether of agreement or disputation . . .'[42] (The design sketched on the table seems in fact to have been the frontispiece for Hone's *Political Showman*.)

Disputation there very likely was. In the year of Peterloo, Cruikshank did caricatures sympathetic to the persecuted reformers, but also (for the conservative George Humphrey, Hannah's successor in St James's Street) a number attacking the hideous, ragged, ignorant, rapacious, devilish radicals, would-be subverters of all that Britons held dear. Some of these were devised by Humphrey; but the two prints in that year on which Cruikshank troubled to put *invt* after his name (*invenit* = he designed it) were both anti-reform. In some cases he seems to have been delighting, as Gillray had done, in carrying to extremes his depiction of the perilous lower orders. But he was also expressing his own fears. The privileged and the merely well-to-do were shaken by the events of 1819 and 1820. It was not excessive to fear revolution. When Cruikshank saw the enormous impact of the pamphlets he illustrated for Hone and of other radical work he did then, such as his *Political 'A Apple Pie'*, he may well have wondered if he was acting wisely: the sharper his satire, the more dangerous it must be. At any rate, when George IV's court sent a go-between to him, about the time that the err-

Detail from 'Coriolanus Addressing the Plebians', published by Humphrey in February 1820. This is a crowd of reformist 'curs' cowering back from a Shakespearian dressing-down delivered by George IV in front of his palace, Carlton House. On left, extreme radicals; then William Cobbett, holding the bones of Thomas Paine; Henry Hunt, radical orator; little Thomas Jonathan Wooler, editor of the radical *Black Dwarf*; Major John Cartwright, veteran reformer: John Cam Hobhouse and Sir Francis Burdett (who were elected the following month as radical MPs for Westminster); Alderman Waithman, radical City MP; William Hone, with clubs labelled 'Parody' and 'Man in the Moon – House that Jack Built'; and Cruikshank himself, with a portfolio of caricatures, looking abashed

ing Queen Caroline returned in early June 1820 from her continental gallivanting to become the reformers' tarnished heroine, Cruikshank was willing to listen. On 19 June he signed a receipt for one hundred pounds of the royal money 'in consideration of a pledge not to caricature His Majesty in any immoral situation'.[43] It is true that other caricaturists and a number of printsellers were getting similar large bribes from the king to shield him from ridicule, and Robert Cruikshank had taken seventy pounds the month before to suppress a caricature of the king called 'The Dandy of Sixty'; but it is most unlikely that George dared to confess his one hundred pounds to Hone. It was easy for him to keep the secret, for the word 'immoral' in the pledge let him feel free to go on exposing the king to ridicule (for example, being sold as cat's-meat, or being grilled by devils, in later Hone pamphlets).

What must have vexed Hone, however, was to see Cruikshank not

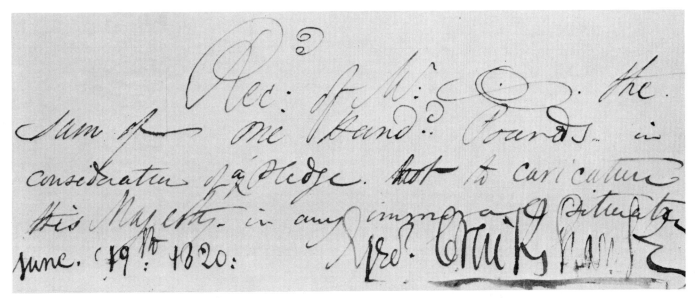

Cruikshank's receipt, in the Royal Archives. Reproduced by gracious permission of Her Majesty the Queen

only persisting with anti-reform caricatures for Humphrey right through the intense conflict over Queen Caroline, but even doing ten for *The Loyalist's Magazine*, a weekly set up late in 1820 to brighten up the Tory counter-attack. There was always the consolation for Hone, though, that such things never sold as well as his own. *The Loyalist's Magazine* complained, 'While everything against Government is bought up with avidity . . . through every corner of the land . . . the loyal and worthiest part of the community are culpably remiss in purchasing and distributing loyal pamphlets to counteract the poison.' Every time Hone issued a new pamphlet his shop was blockaded with buyers. He claimed that in two years he sold about 250,000 copies, and there were a dozen other men busy at the same work. The outrage of *The Loyalist's Magazine* is typical of the Tory response: 'There never has existed a parallel, in the memory of the present age, of such gross abuse and ridicule, such mendaciousness and falsehood, as have been mercilessly heaped upon the King by the Radical Press . . . To what is all this tending? To drive on the multitude blindly and rashly to the very edge of the fearful precipice.'[44]

Hone was paid the compliment of being singled out for abuse. As a self-made literary man, he was probably hurt most by jibes at his verses. One attacker tells him he was wise to make 'a flash bargain with a wag . . . to aid your threadbare talent' –

> For who, in fits at Cruiky's droll designs,
> Can stay to criticize lopsided lines?
> Make much of that droll dog, and feed him fat . . .[45]

This looks like an attempt to drive a wedge between the two men, based perhaps on knowledge of some strain between them. Cruikshank had

not been fed fat: for seventy-eight wood engravings (mostly fairly simple things, it is true) he got sixty pounds, and the vast sales must have brought Hone thousands. Quite likely it was already known, in the small world of London publishing, that Cruikshank was inclined to imagine himself undervalued; and Hone was not a man to undervalue himself. He says in a letter to Francis Douce, the scholar and collector, that a frontispiece Cruikshank had just done for Hone's *Right Divine of Kings to Govern Wrong* (see page 95) 'is a thing of my own (as indeed all my *cuts* are)'.[46] A few years later Hone wrote: 'My little pieces acquainted every rank of society in the most remote corner of the British dominions with the powers of Mr George Cruikshank, whose genius had been wasted on mere caricature till it embodied my ideas and feelings. When his brother artists, and everyone who had the least judgment, praised the multiform fertility of the freest pencil that ever drew a line on a block, it began to be appreciated by publishers.'[47] Hone's pamphlets had indeed much extended the artist's fame; but Hone is unjust in thus slighting the earlier work.

In a pamphlet of 1821, *The Radical. Chiefs*, there was more wedge-driving mockery of the self-taught Hone and his verse:

> It would not one poor shilling from us stir
> Did not friend Cruiky just in time occur
> To frame a woodcut to explain the sense . . .
> Ah! were I Cruikshank, I w'd write myself
> And not to schemer H--e give all the pelf.

Such talk did nothing to break their friendship. The same pamphlet may have had some effect, though, in a passage that urged Cruikshank to atone for his attacks on George IV:

> Now clear away the filth you rashly threw
> And give his unstain'd visage to our view.[48]

Cruikshank was now at a turning-point; and it happens that a clue to the state of his mind can be found in *The Radical Chiefs*. As a frontispiece the pamphlet has a folding caricature showing an array of reformers, radical and not so radical, all with revolutionary red bonnets, ranging from William Cobbett, T. J. Wooler (editor of *The Black Dwarf*), Richard Carlile (jailed editor of *The Republican*) and Arthur Thistlewood (recently executed for treason) over to Byron's friend John Cam Hobhouse, and Sir Francis Burdett, MP. In the centre, at a table resting on a box labelled 'Gunpowder in boxwood' (an allusion to the power of the wood engravings), sits Hone, armed with pistols, holding up a sheet headed 'Parody'. A guillotine stands behind him, and he is saying, 'No king, no church, no order on the face of the earth.' Beside him stands Robert Cruikshank: the creator of this caricature. He says, 'Much may be said on both sides.' Next to him sits George, holding a giant pencil and looking at a sheet headed 'Black designs'. A paper marked Anarchy lies at his feet. He spits into an upturned royal crown and says, 'Damn all things'.

It is an unexpected detail to find in a loyalist publication (issued by William Turner, Stationer to His Majesty). Robert Cruikshank seems to be both injecting some mockery into the job he is doing for the loyalists, and perpetrating something of a joke against his brother. Yet there would be no point in it if 'Damn all things' were not a thought then in George's mind.

There is some reason to think that George was in a cynical, erratic state at this period – say, 1819–22. Taking a bribe from the crown is not likely to have been an act he was at ease with in the sterner part of his mind, the part from his mother. Gillray had gone much further and accepted a pension (from Pitt in 1797 – reported in *The Scourge* in 1812); did Cruikshank wonder about its effect on Gillray's work, and perhaps on his nerves? He seems to have had fits of self-doubt or gloom. William Clarke gives a tantalising glimpse of him in 1821: 'When George and I used to set-to together (he always sparred upon the defensive) he would say very coolly after a busy bout, "I think I shall die in about two years time."'[49] Hone was finding him a troublesome colleague. In a letter dated January 1821 he says he will not be able to get on with his work unless 'my friend Cruikshank will forswear late hours, blue ruin [gin] and dollies', which make him unreliable. Hone says that when he complains to Cruikshank, he answers 'to the purport or effect following: "You be d----d" or "Go to hell", or else when he hath been less under the influence of "daffy" [gin], he has invited me in rather a dictatorial tone to "Go and teach my granny to suck eggs!" This demoniac possession is on him even now –' George is demanding that Hone should go instantly to an alderman he knows to seek the dismissal of a constable with whom George has apparently clashed while on a spree. When Hone

refused, George 'blew clouds of tobacco smoke over me and my books... demanded entrance to my wife's bedroom to shave and smarten himself up for an evening party, took possession of my best Brandenburg pumps ... and manifested what I have long suspected, that he is by no means friendly to Reform!'[50]

A letter to Hone six months later from a staunch reformer, Leigh Hunt's brother John, suggests that by then Hone as well as Cruikshank was felt to need some pushing. John Hunt was serving a year in Cold Bath Fields Prison, Clerkenwell, for having said in *The Examiner* that the House of Commons was 'for the main part . . . composed of venal borough-mongers, grasping placemen, greedy adventurers, and aspiring title-hunters . . . a far greater proportion of public criminals than public guardians . . .' George IV was about to be crowned, all on his own, although his wife Caroline was embarrassingly in town and was insisting, with the support of Whigs and radicals, on being crowned with him. After a call from William Hazlitt (visiting hours 11.30 am–2 pm), Hunt wrote to Hone: 'What are you about? I saw Mr Hazlitt today; and asking him whether you were at work on the coronation, he said he did not know. How is this? Here is what I should call a golden opportunity for you and your friend Cruikshank . . . There will perhaps be fifty or sixty thousand people in town from the country, all wanting something to carry home with them of the droll kind . . . Rouse up, there is time for *something* even now.'[51]

Hone and Cruikshank disappointed him. However, they had been busy on something else. A couple of weeks after the coronation Hone published a sardonic parody of a new kind: not a caricature or a pamphlet, but a newspaper, *A Slap at Slop* (see page 98). The coronation is one target among many, dismissed as a tomfoolery that makes John Bull stare while the Chancellor of the Exchequer picks his pocket (it cost £243,000). *A Slap at Slop* was a great success; and yet it was to be Hone's last radical publication. Within a year of bemoaning Cruikshank's lack of reforming zeal, Hone himself abandoned political work. Cruikshank's turn away from politics was only to take a little longer.

Hone's reputation, however, thanks to endless Tory abuse, continued to match the picture that Robert Cruikshank had drawn of him. Sometimes he managed to be amused by it; in 1822 he wrote a sketch in which a woman who comes to his shop is astonished to learn that the harmless-looking man facing her is Hone himself: '... Why, indeed, sir, I did not suppose I should *see* you – and I did not expect – (*embarrassed*) – that is, I thought – I expected – I – I –' 'Allow me, madam, to conclude: you expected I had horns and hoofs, a forked tail, and spouted fire?'[52]

And it looks as if this is the sort of picture that George Cruikshank's mother had of Hone, and that she accused him of leading her son astray. In July 1822 she wrote to Hone (from a new home in the suburb of Pentonville) a letter whose drift is evident enough from Hone's weighty reply (he kept a copy). He said: 'Whatever of kindness I entertain, and I entertain much, for your son George, has been from admiration of his talents and respect for his honourable disposition. For everything that could diminish either of those qualities, I have expressed to him not only deep regret, but remonstrated with him more severely than anyone but a sincere friend, feeling deeply for his best interests and real welfare, would venture to do. If he has, as you say, left your house for three years, you must be better acquainted with the reason for his seeking a home elsewhere than I am.'[53] His closing phrase is bound to reflect some knowledge of how things stood between mother and son. Perhaps possessiveness was her chief flaw. At the age of almost thirty, George was daring to escape the maternal eye! She was very likely worried, of course, about the blue ruin and dollies; and especially the blue ruin. When George had left home in 1819, perhaps it was after having been berated once too often about coming home in drink. Hone's opening sentences say tactfully that he has been trying to restrain George; and the recollections of one of Hone's daughters, a Mrs Burn, are interesting on this point: 'Our mother and father sought to draw him from the loose companionship he indulged in, by keeping him at home in the evenings, and often to sleep – he was the only one our mother ever had a bed made up for.'[54]

Hone could have suggested to Mrs Cruikshank that she might direct her complaints elsewhere: to the theatre people, journalists and men of the flash sporting world with whom George was seeing life. It was in 1820–1, in the midst of his work for the pamphleteers, and when Hone was complaining about his late nights, that George collaborated with his brother and Pierce Egan, the leading sporting journalist of the day, on a publication utterly free of political content. This, his first important non-caricature work, was *Life in London, or The Day and Night Scenes of Jerry Hawthorn Esq and His Elegant Friend Corinthian Tom, accompanied by Bob Logic, the Oxonian, in Their Rambles and Sprees Through the Metropolis.* Its enormous success, first in monthly instalments, then as a book, and even more in a dozen stage versions, can be ascribed mainly to its slice-of-life quality. It took its heroes through thirty-six 'scenes from real life,' alternating between the fashionable West End and the haunts of sporting men, prostitutes and beggars. For readers of all ranks it offered an adroit blend of the familar and the unfamiliar; a guided tour to the pleasures and dissipations of London; some moral cautions; and a running lesson from Egan in the slang of the underworld and of sporting gentlemen. The author of the most successful stage version, W. T. Moncrieff, recalled, 'Dukes and dustmen were equally interested in its performance, and peers might be seen mobbing it with apprentices to obtain an admission.' It was denounced as a guide to immorality; the Methodists, says Moncrieff, 'distributed the whole of the stock of the Religious Tract Society at the doors of the theatre.'[55]

The Cruikshank illustrations offered many pleasures of recognition. The cadgers (see page 102), for instance, were people whom Londoners could see on their streets. Several scenes show George Cruikshank's fascination with the anarchic tumult of humble people at play – scenes with which his father had been familiar but which his mother must have despised and feared. According to Moncrieff, who knew the Cruikshank

brothers, the three leading characters, Tom, Jerry and Logic, were derived from George and Robert Cruikshank and Pierce Egan, and many of the adventures in the book were in part autobiographical. Certainly George's rambles and sprees with his brother and his friends must have made their contribution. But George was soon in two minds about the achievement. He told the author of the biographical sketch of 1834 that the idea 'originated entirely' with himself, but he had 'intended to paint a series of pictures on the subject, after the manner of Hogarth, and to be called *Life* in London is *Death*' and 'he still regrets that the moral he intended to convey . . . was not represented on the stage.'[56] In later life he kept returning to and elaborating this point. To quote one of his biographers, William Bates: 'The story is, as he has often related it to myself and others, that George, who was even then a moralist, either had misconceived the object of the author, or saw that his designs were used for a purpose he had not contemplated; and finding that the book, which created a perfect furore, was a guide to, rather than a dissuasion from, the vicious haunts and amusements of the metropolis, retired from the firm.'[57] Both these stories, however, demonstrate something of the gap between the younger and the older Cruikshank. When *Life in London* was at the height of its fame, he certainly did not renounce it. On the contrary: months after the printed version was complete, and when Moncrieff's and other stage versions were in full swing (and being attacked by moralists), George collaborated with Egan in yet another stage production. It opened at Sadler's Wells on 8 April 1822 with the following flourish:

The New Pedestrian-Equestrian Extravaganza and Operatic Burletta, in Three Acts of Gaiety, Frisk, Lark and Patter, called Tom and Jerry, or Life in London.

George painted some of the scenery, according to the programme: 'The sporting subjects by Mr G. Cruikshank, from Designs by himself and Brother.' And when the songs from this burletta were published, they were 'embellished with a highly finished coloured plate of the pony races . . . by Mr George Cruikshank'. These races were part of the show, run by real ponies on raised platforms extending from the stage, round the sides of the pit and back again. They really understood theatre-in-the-round in those days.

It is true that there was a moral to the show. The last scene of the burletta is summarized like this: 'Jerry's symptoms of uneasiness – cracked heads – debilitated – out of wind – can't come to time; and the constitution fast on the decline – Logic lumbered – and Tom *done up* – portraying that LIFE IN LONDON, without the check-string, is a rapid trot towards Death! Jerry sees his folly . . .'[58] That message was already there in the original; but George may have had a hand in emphasizing it. A change in his way of life was near: a change associated with new developments in his work.

A few hundred yards north of Sadler's Wells, the New River Company had begun a housing estate that was soon to fill in almost the last remaining fields between the expanding metropolis and the villages of Pentonville and Islington. The gracious Georgian houses were aimed at well-to-do people. In 1820, when the first terrace was still uncompleted, Mrs Cruikshank took No. 11 in it, at fifty pounds a year plus rates (more than many families had to keep themselves on). It still stands, now No. 11 Claremont Square – a house of basement and four floors, like the old home in Dorset Street. She must have intended George to move in with her, for Robert was now married and established elsewhere, and the only other child was a thirteen-year-old daughter. One likely purpose of the move was to improve the health of this girl, who had only five years to live – for the district was high and airy and had several small medicinal spas. Mrs Cruikshank may well also have wanted to put a mile and a half between George and his late-night haunts. In this she was disappointed for two years or more, as her complaint to Hone shows. But George appears to have moved in by 1823; and then to have married soon afterwards and moved, in 1824, to another just-completed house fourteen doors to the south.

Of George's first wife little can be discovered except that her name was Mary Ann, that she had no children, and that she died of tuberculosis at Ealing, presumably in a sanitorium, in May 1849 at the age of forty-two. If the marriage was in 1824 she was then seventeen. A homebody is suggested in a passing reference to her in the William Clarke article of 1833: Clarke says that Cruikshank 'resembles us in having a remarkably pleasant little wife – one who makes most poetical and accurate tea' (she brings the pot to the kettle the moment it is boiling).[59] It is remarkable that no later writer mentions her. Did his second wife (whom he married within ten months) object to hearing her spoken of? Did he feel guilty about her illness and death? A draft letter of his from the 1830s says she is in 'a dreadful nervous state of health'.[60] Whether her nerves drove him back to the taverns, or his drinking upset her nerves, it is impossible to say.

The question of his drinking is a difficult one. He is described as a high-spirited tavern companion, a great singer of ballads and teller of stories accompanied by comical gesticulation. He belonged to several tavern-based clubs, beginning with the one that had been his father's, The Brilliants, which became The Eccentrics and migrated to the Crown Tavern in Vinegar Yard off Drury Lane. Among his fellow-members there were Moncrieff and a noted comic actor, Robert Keeley, who played in the Drury Lane and Sadler's Wells versions of *Life in London*. Another was The Crib, of which Joe Grimaldi was a leading member. It met at the Sir Hugh Myddelton's Head near the Sadler's Wells Theatre, and thus a few minutes' walk from Cruikshank's new home. Then there was The Maidenhead, a public house in the opposite direction, near what is now King's Cross Station, kept by William Walbourn, a cockney actor who had a great success as Dusty Bob in *Life in London*. Cruikshank etched a portrait print of him and painted him as Dusty Bob for a new sign for his house; and evidently belonged to another club there,

for on 4 November 1825 Walbourn wrote to Egan: '. . . i shall fele greately oblidged if you will serve me by teaking the chear on wenesday next if convnt you will oblidge me Mr Cruickshank as promis to [?appear].'[61] Another letter gives a glimpse of Cruikshank's bachelor days. A man named H. T. Bradish writes in December 1824 about his job-hunting, says he will soon be 'todling to take a peep at you', and ends:

Green grow the rushes O
There was a time when you and I———
! ! ! ! ! ! ! ! ! !
Were loved by all the lassies O![62]

There was a time: but now he is married. Through the 1820s and 1830s there is no firm evidence that he was an excessive drinker. Certainly the quantity and quality of his work does not suggest it. In 1829 he published the first of several etchings on the evils of gin (of course it might be argued that these were works of remorse). A man who knew him in the 1840s, W. H. Wills, wrote, 'Surely no man drank with more fervour and enjoyment, nor carried his liquor so kindly, so merrily. Then was the time to hear him sing "Lord Bateman" in character.'[63] (This was a comically cockneyfied version of an old ballad, which Dickens annotated and Cruikshank illustrated.) That does not suggest a real drunkard. Yet Henry Vizetelly, whose father was one of Cruikshank's publishers, wrote in 1893: 'Somewhere in the Forties . . . drink had so far got the mastery over him that he was pretty constantly in police custody during the small hours of the morning, having been either found in the street in an insensible condition . . . or been taken in charge for his personal protection.'[64] It may be that a few incidents had given him an over-dramatic reputation. One sure fact is that in July 1847 he took the pledge of abstinence of which he was thereafter constantly reminding the world; and it is worth noting that Mary Ann's tuberculosis had been medically confirmed in 1847.[65] Was his teetotalism in part an act of penance?

His turn to domesticity in 1823 was paralleled in his work. Since 1813 he had been the leading caricaturist not only in quality but also (on the evidence of the work that survives) in output, with Rowlandson and Charles Williams at first his only near rivals, and then only his brother. In 1823 he was surpassed by his brother and by a newcomer, William Heath. His turning away from politics is particularly striking. In 1820 he had done (if all his wood engravings for pamphlets are counted) nearly two-hundred political caricatures; in the five years 1823–7 the numbers are eight, seven, four, three, one. There was, it is true, an easing of political controversy in those years, but no such change as that. More striking still is Cruikshank's response to the struggle over reform that gripped the nation during 1830–2. In those three years, when the fate of the abuses that he had formerly attacked was being decided, 1,165 political caricatures are recorded, but only two are by him. The change had been in himself.

From 1823 a growing proportion of his work was on a small scale, about three inches by two – a scale in which he had had intensive practice in his pamphlet wood engravings. The message, however, was no longer 'gunpowder in boxwood'. He was working to give pleasure at the fireside and in the nursery. In 1822–3 he did eight delicate etchings for *Peter Schlemihl*, the story of the boy who sold his shadow, and ten for the first English edition of the Grimm fairy tales – etchings that established him on the continent as well as in England as a masterly fairy-tale illustrator. He also did ten small etchings and eight wood engravings for a compilation by his friend William Clarke, *Points of Humour*. This book is notable as the occasion of the first long article in praise of Cruikshank, by Walter Scott's son-in-law J. G. Lockhart in *Blackwood's Magazine*.

Lockhart's Scottish enthusiasm was aroused in particular by a series of illustrations in the book to Burns's *Jolly Beggars* (see page 110); but he was also intent on exhorting Cruikshank to take himself more seriously: 'It is high time that the public should think more than they have hitherto done of George Cruikshank; and it is also high time that George Cruikshank should begin to think more than he seems to have done hitherto of himself. Generally speaking, people consider him as a clever, sharp caricaturist, and nothing more – a free-handed, comical young fellow, who will do anything he is paid for, and who is quite contented to dine off the proceeds of a ''George IV'' [caricature] today, and those of a ''Hone'' or a ''Cobbett'' tomorrow. He himself, indeed, appears to be the most careless creature alive, as touching his reputation. He seems to have no plan – almost no ambition . . . He does just what is suggested . . . pockets the cash – orders his beefsteak and bowl – and chaunts, like one of his own heroes,

> Life is all a variorum,
> We regard not how it goes.'

It is time to pull up, says Lockhart: 'Perhaps he is not aware of the fact himself – but a fact it undoubtedly is – that he possesses genius – GENIUS in its truest sense – strong, original English genius . . . He draws with the ease, and freedom, and fearlessness of a master . . . but let him do himself justice – let him persevere and *rise* in his own path . . . let him think of Hogarth.'

Lockhart then presumes to advise Cruikshank, one of the most industrious of men, how he should spend his day. 'He should be indefatigable in reading – and the time to begin is 6 am. What a breakfast he will be able to devour about nine or half-past nine . . ! Then let him draw, etch and paint until about two o'clock pm, then take a lounge through the streets to see if anything is stirring – step into Westminster Hall [for the law courts] – the fives court, the Rev Edward Irving's chapel . . . or any other public place, jotting down à la Hogarth all the absurd faces he falls in with upon his fingernails. A slight dinner and a single bottle will carry him on till it is time to go to the play, or the Castle Tavern [a boxers' rendezvous in Holborn], or the House of Commons . . .' This is Lockhart's final advice: 'Cruikshank may, if he pleases, be a second Gillray; but, once more, this should not be his ambition. He is fitted for a higher walk. Let him . . . pick up his pocket-money by Gillrayizing; but let him give his days and his nights to labour that Gillray's shoulders were not meant for.'[66]

The advice against Gillrayizing was already becoming unnecessary. And he did not need to be told to have a high opinion of himself or to emulate Hogarth or any other master. In the 1820s the newly-married householder in his thirties was concerned with achieving some kind of independence. If he had turned away from his old role of the freelance artist bringing his ideas to printsellers, was he to survive and express himself and gain the world's esteem only by illustrating the work of others?

His first attempt to break free was *Phrenological Illustrations*, published in 1826 'by George Cruikshank, Myddelton Terrace, Pentonville . . . 8 shillings plain, 12 shillings coloured'. It does not take a higher walk. It consists of six large oblong folio sheets of etchings, bound together, jokily illustrating the thirty-three human characteristics that the phrenologists Gall and Spurzheim claimed to be able to deduce from the surface of the cranium: amativeness, combativeness, and so on (see page 123). Cruikshank sent a review copy to his old friend Hone, now bankrupt and living 'within the rules' of King's Bench Prison in Southwark – that is, in a designated house nearby – but managing to produce a monthly magazine, *The Every-Day Book*. Hone gave Cruikshank a four-page puff, and said, 'His inimitable powers have hitherto entertained and delighted the public far more to the emolument of others than himself; and now that he has ventured to ''take a benefit'' on his account, there cannot be a doubt that his admirers will encourage ''their old favourite'' to successive endeavours . . . His entire talents have never been called forth . . .' He adds that all booksellers in London and throughout the kingdom have the work, 'yet it would be a well-timed compliment to Mr Cruikshank if town purchasers . . . were to direct their steps to his house, No 25, Myddelton Terrace, Pentonville'.[67]

What would an admirer have seen who took Hone's hint, or who made the expedition to buy one of the similar works he published in the next six years? No. 25 (now 69 Amwell Street) was and is a simple Georgian terrace house of basement and three floors, each of two rooms, one of which served as Cruikshank's studio. To the east, from the front windows, could be seen the rapidly growing streets of similar or larger houses. The back windows looked down a long slope to the valley of the Fleet River. Near the bottom there were tile-kilns, but there was also a large expanse of gardens – 'the solitary spot in Clerkenwell to which the rage for building has not as yet extended,' said a writer of 1828. 'From Gray's Inn Lane . . . on the opposite side of the valley, the view of Myddelton Gardens, with the little summer-houses attached to many of them, has a pleasing effect.'[68] Cruikshank was soon to see the slope built over.

Down beside the Fleet, the once-famous pleasure resort and tea-gardens of Bagnigge Wells had been closed for some years and stripped of their temple, arbours, lead statues and two hundred tables. But there was much else to make the walk from town worth while. From his back windows Cruikshank could see to the left Islington Spa, also optimistically known as New Tunbridge Wells – created round a spring whose water was held to restore the appetite and cure nervous disorders. At Sadler's Wells there was another spa, and the Sir Hugh Myddelton's Head had tea-gardens and a skittle-ground. The theatre itself had just extended its season from six months to twelve, as the neighbourhood population had grown so much. And a quarter-mile to the north of Myddelton Terrace was yet another popular resort of what Londoners called merry Islington: White Conduit House, with large gardens, bowling-greens, tea-rooms, dancing, concerts – and a reputation for lowness and immorality. It had been surrounded by fields, but they too were filling with houses. A little further still, though, up winding Hagbush Lane, there was rural peace. 'The wild onion, clowns-woundwort, wake-robin and abundance of other simples, lovely in their form and of high medicinal repute . . . seed and flower here in great variety,' says *The Every-Day Book*. 'How long beneath the tall elms and pollard oaks . . . the infirm may be suffered to seek health, and the healthy to recreate, who shall say? Spoilers are abroad.'[69]

In 1833, another old acquaintance of Cruikshank's, William Clarke, paid tribute to him in the article quoted earlier – the longest so far written on him, a fifteen-page piece in the *Monthly Magazine* (issued, it must be said, by Charles Tilt, one of Cruikshank's publishers). Clarke calls Cruikshank 'our second Hogarth'; but he is little known, for he 'keeps snug'. 'His deportment, generally speaking, is severe; his glance bites like aqua-fortis. As he passes through the streets, nobody knows, nobody notices him. He hears the ready laugh at one of his pictorial effusions in a shop-window, mentally curses the engraver who has spoiled his design [this would be a wood engraving], and passes on gravely as though he were going to a funeral.'

Cruikshank briefed Clarke to make a point he often insisted on: 'We can confidently assert that George never keeps a notebook – and rarely takes a sketch from nature. His elder brother Robert *books* every queer head "he comes across" [the earliest recorded use of this phrase]. George, however, trusts to the ample stores of memory. Even that felicitous portrait of Rounding, the Epping Huntsman, which is recognized at a glance . . . was drawn "at sixty days after sight".'[70] But it happens that on this very portrait of Tom Rounding, for Thomas Hood's poem *The Epping Hunt* in 1829, there is some evidence the other way. A son of the printseller Thomas Tegg recalled this of Cruikshank: 'When he had no paper I have known him to make notes and even sketches on his thumb nail. This he did in the case of the portrait of Tom Rounding' – at a dinner party with Rounding and Hood.[71] The truth probably is that Cruikshank had a knack of recall on which he rightly prided himself, but his vanity made him exaggerate – even though he must have known that his hero Gillray carried sketch-cards with him. In 1811, it will be remembered, Cruikshank pictured himself holding pencil and sketch-

book; and in 1822 his brother shows him with sketch-cards in his hand.[72]

Clarke gives an explanation, presumably from the master, of Cruikshank's turning away from political caricature. When George Canning came to power, he says, 'George was floored'. He must mean in 1822, when Canning re-entered the government after Castlereagh's suicide, and not 1827, when he became prime minister. 'He could not render popular and comparatively speaking liberal ministers . . . pictorially ridiculous,' Clarke goes on; 'he loved popular liberality, and the same feeling so completely sways him at this moment that he would not point a pencil against our present monarch [William IV] or Earl Grey, or Baron Brougham, for the universe . . . In this dilemma he proposed to illustrate books.'[73] It is true that after 1822 the government was less extreme in its toryism; but after 1830 why did Cruikshank do no more than two caricatures for the more popular and liberal Whigs? Part of the answer does seem to be that he had become a non-enthusiast for reform. Six months after Clarke's article, the Tory *Fraser's Magazine* wrote, recalling Cruikshank's work of 1820, 'We Tory folk were horribly angry at the time . . . We rather think he quitted ere long the shabby crew who wished to make him their property, and has settled down, if not into the genuine faith of a Tory, at least into that approach to orthodoxy which consists

This is a capital portrait of George:—and although done some years ago it is still delightfully like him. An hour ago, George Cruikshank was sitting opposite us, pencil in hand; at this moment, with a trifling difference in apparel and mustachio, gentle reader, if you will condescend to fancy yourself Hone, and *mosaic* yourself into the engraving, George Cruikshank will sit opposite you.

Cruikshank's sketch of Hone and himself working on a pamphlet. He drew it for a re-issue of his pamphlets by Hone in 1827. William Clarke used the woodblock again in his article of 1833 (see this page), and here it is reproduced with Clarke's commentary in the detestation of a Whig.' And *Fraser's* wishes Cruikshank would 'wake a little' and depict 'the humours and stupidities of whiggism'.[74]

Perhaps he let different interviewers deduce what they wished of his politics. Eight years later, a book of contemporary biographies says, 'Not only is he a decided Liberal, but his Liberalism has with him all the authority of a moral law . . . No consideration on earth . . . would prevail on him to caricature, however harmlessly, any of those statesmen whose political views he shares.'[75] The truth is, neither Whig nor Tory needed to fear Cruikshank's pencil after the last token efforts of 1831. Nor was the folly or scandalous behaviour of any particular lord, lady or other eminent person pointed at after the mid-1820s. His fantasy was confined to more sociable inventions. He became respectable; it would be difficult to argue that his art benefited. In the 1830s, it is true, he did scores of good illustrations for other men's books, but in the folios he published in his own name, as an assertion of his independence as an artist, he is too often merely whimsical, didactic or facetious-genteel. He began to get a reputation for combativeness and discontent. Perhaps he felt trapped; in servitude to publishers. The *Fraser's Magazine* article says, 'Of course, George is, like all men of undoubted genius, a most ill-used gentleman . . . shocked at the evil fate which consigns him to drawing sketches and caricatures, instead of letting him loose in his natural domain of epic or historical picture.'[76] (In 1830 he had had an oil painting accepted at the Royal Academy, a scene from *The Vicar of Wakefield* entitled 'Fitting Out Moses for the Fair'; but he did not exhibit again until 1852.)

The Clarke article ends with a promise of a sequel the following month containing, among other things, 'a consideration of George's occasional failures and incapacities; his devout aspirations to quit the ludicrous, which he condemns, for the sublime, which he admires; his extraordinary powers, considering the paucity of his academical acquirements; his fancy and invention; his Scraps and Sketches, in which the full extent of his ability is shown – for in them he is neither fettered by the conceptions of authors nor the punctilios of publishers; the history of his attempting to paint in oil, from his earliest efforts; . . . his days of toil over faces "no bigger than peas", which to the unconscious public seem to have been hit off "at a moment's notice" . . . '[77] This sequel did not appear. It would have told us something about Cruikshank's uneasy middle-aged search for a satisfying role. Perhaps Clarke was threatening to touch on too many conflicts and uncertainties, and Cruikshank rebelled.

Cruikshank had been right in seeing, some years before the reign of Victoria began, that the society in which the printshop caricature trade had flourished was giving way to one that set more value on decorum and on useful literature. Two years before Victoria came to the throne, an event occurred that serves to mark the close of an era. Following the death of Hannah Humphrey's successor, her nephew George, an auction was held of the contents of the shop at 27 St James's Street where since 1797 the caricatures of Gillray and then (though less copiously) of Cruikshank had graced the windows. From July 13 to 16, 1835, everything went: thousands of caricatures and hundreds of drawings by Gillray, Cruikshank and others; hundreds of their copperplates; a number of suppressed prints and plates; thirteen bound volumes containing 2,157 caricatures collected by Charles James Fox; two parcels of Gillray's correspondence, including many suggestions for caricatures 'from the most eminent men of his time'; the cupboards and counters from which countless thousands of caricatures had been sold; and even the windows of the shop 'and the prints on the sashes'.[78] Cruikshank was busy with the launching of a publication of the kind that was superseding caricature prints in the popular market – the monthly *Comic Almanack*; but he did not forget the shop of Gillray his master, where he himself had first been welcomed a quarter-century before. In an act of homage, he bought Gillray's work-table, and he kept it all his life.[79] But none of the work he created on it in the next forty years would have reminded admirers of Gillray that this man had once been his heir.

By 1835 the independent caricature print was becoming a minor amusement. A political and moral change was not the sole cause of this decline. It was accelerated by the growth of many forms of low-cost publishing. In the 1820s the March of Intellect had been proclaimed. It was a time of 'useful knowledge to the people' and quick-coming inventions. When the fast-growing reading public was not seeking useful information, it wanted novelties. To new men in the trade, the etched print with its limited run must have seemed a relic of the unadmirable eighteenth century. A shop could no longer live by caricatures alone; an artist still less so. One innovation that directly undermined the caricature print was the weekly paper illustrated with wood engravings and selling for only a penny. Another development – one that affected the tone of caricatures – was the widespread substitution, around 1830, of lithography for etching. The softened images of the lithograph admirably suited the general turning-away from satiric savagery.

Some men born soon enough to remember the printshop windows in their days of scurrilous glory lamented the change. One of these was William Makepeace Thackeray, who was nine at the time of the Queen Caroline trial, and who as a young man took lessons from Cruikshank. In 1840 Thackeray paid tribute to Cruikshank in a long illustrated article in the *Westminster Review*. He grieved genially over the printshops of his boyhood: 'Knight's, in Sweeting's Alley; Fairburn's, in a court off Ludgate Hill; Hone's, in Fleet Street – bright, enchanted palaces, which George Cruikshank used to people with grinning, fantastical imps and merry, harmless sprites – where are they? Fairburn's shop knows him no more; not only has Knight disappeared from Sweeting's Alley, but, as we are given to understand, Sweeting's Alley has disappeared from the face of the globe. Slop, the atrocious Castlereagh, the sainted Caroline . . . the Dandy of Sixty, who used to glance at us from Hone's friendly windows – where are they? Mr Cruikshank may have drawn a thousand better things, since the days when these were; but they are to us a thousand times more pleasing than anything else he has done. How we used to believe in them! to stray miles out of the way on holidays, in order to ponder for an hour before that delightful window in Sweeting's Alley! in walks through Fleet Street, to vanish abruptly down Fairburn's passage, and there make one at his "charming gratis" exhibition! There used to be a crowd round the window in those days of grinning good-natured mechanics, who spelt the songs and spoke them out for the benefit of the company, and who received the points of humour with a general sympathizing roar. Where are these people now? You never hear any laughing at HB [John Doyle, who led the way in lithographic caricatures]; his pictures are a great deal too genteel for that – polite points of wit which . . . cause one to smile in a quiet, gentlemanlike kind of way.'[80]

Cruikshank too had become by then a man for genteel smiles, though Thackeray does not admit it. He does not take his praise much beyond the 1820s. He calls Cruikshank 'the friend of the young especially', and recalls having as a boy given up tarts to buy Cruikshank prints: among them, when he was fifteen, the *Phrenological Illustrations*, 'which entire work was purchased by a joint stock company of boys, each drawing lots afterwards for the separate prints'.[81] Gillray had hardly been 'the friend of the young', and many caricatures by him and his contemporaries, and by the early Cruikshank, were most questionable fare for children. Thackeray himself made this point in an article fourteen years later on the pleasant domestic art of John Leech, the *Punch* artist. Thackeray recalls from his childhood the portfolios of caricatures in his grandfather's house, and says, 'But if our sisters wanted to look at the portfolios, the good old grandfather used to hesitate. There were some prints among them very odd indeed; some that girls could not under-stand; some that boys, indeed, had best not see. We swiftly turn over those prohibited pages. How many of them there were in the wild, coarse, reckless, ribald, generous book of old English humour!' By this date Cruikshank had been several years a teetotaller and was not even creating many genteel laughs suitable for all the family. Good-hearted Thackeray complains gently: 'He has rather deserted satire and comedy of late years, having turned his attention to the serious, and warlike, and sublime . . . We prefer the comic and fanciful.'[82]

The ageing Cruikshank could not see it like that. In 1860, when he was beginning work on his vast 'Triumph of Bacchus', he wrote in his own entry for a biographical dictionary: 'All his life he has (we believe) had a strong desire to attain to the higher branches of his profession – but never had time or opportunity to study – the proverb however of "never too late to learn" may be applied in this instance – for despite of all difficulties he has for the last few years employed himself principally in oil painting . . . His later pictures show that he bids fair to stand – as he has all his life desired to stand, viz, as an *Oil Painter* as well as an *Etcher* – and we doubt not but that his oil pictures & his water color drawings will be as much valued & sought after as his etchings are.'[83]

It was not to be. Already he could see his early work being sold in printshops for many times what it had cost in the days of Fores and Fairburn. But his paintings soon slipped from view. The one to which he devoted most time and passion – the *Triumph of Bacchus*, centrepiece of his 1863 exhibition – has lain unseen for years among other sequestered embarrassments of the Tate Gallery. That is no outrage. George Cruik-shank's public was and is right in finding that he lives in his satire and his comedy, and especially in the reckless, ribald, generous work of the earlier years, before he became a Victorian.

A NOTE ON THE PRINTS

The work reproduced here begins with the year of Trafalgar and extends beyond the passing of the first Reform Bill: more than a quarter-century of turbulent British history. In 1805 the nineteenth century had only haltingly begun; by the 1830s the scene was set for Victoria. George Cruikshank watched what was going on, laughed and fumed at it, and had some influence on the way men's thoughts went.

The selection falls into three groups: from boyhood to 1819; the political work of 1819–21; and the period of transition away from print-shop caricatures, stopping short of the founding of the *Comic Almanack* (1835) and the first work for Dickens.

On matters of style, I have let these etchings and wood engravings largely speak for themselves, as I think Cruikshank would have wished. One gets no theorizing from him, except on the study of human anatomy: this, he told the young George Augustus Sala and others, 'will set you all right with your pelvis; and what are you, and what can you do, if your pelvis is wrong?'[84] He began to work in what was, among other things, the Romantic age; and the art-historical eye can detect Romantic elements in him, particularly in his expressive grotesquery. As an illustrator he was one of the pioneers in a great period of English realism: an achievement that owed much to his years as a caricaturist.

It is in their content that caricatures do benefit by some commentary. Some of Cruikshank's finest have had to be put aside, for they dealt with such long-forgotten dramas or were so packed with meanings that they might have been a labour instead of a delight. I have enriched the commentaries that follow with quotations from writings of the day, many of which would have been before Cruikshank's eyes. The result, I hope, is a panorama livelier than an official history of the time, and perhaps full of as many useful truths.

COMICAL YOUNG FELLOW

1805-19

THE WONDERFUL MILL
1805

One of George Cruikshank's earliest surviving prints, done at the age of twelve or thirteen for a minor publisher in Holborn, and sold for a halfpenny. The boy is sure to have been using an existing print for inspiration. It was a long-established fancy to show decrepit men and women tottering to a mill, casting away their crutches and spectacles, and rapidly emerging handsome and young: in the Bodleian Library there is a vast crowded double print of the early eighteenth century, 'The Wonderful Youth Restoring Mill for Grinding Old Women Young (...for Grinding Old Men Young)',[85] in which the new-made young people meet, kiss and dance away.

BONEY BEATING MACK–AND NELSON GIVING HIM A WHACK!!
OR THE BRITISH TARS GIVING BONEY HIS HEART'S DESIRE, SHIPS, COLONIES & COMMERCE
1805

George's father probably helped him with this, but it certainly looks as if the boy (aged thirteen) did most of it. It is George's first work for his father's chief publisher, S. W. Fores of Piccadilly; and his first attempt at Napoleon. The date is 19 November 1805, and George is doing his best to offset the disastrous news, received a fortnight earlier, of the defeat of the British-subsidized Austrians under Mack at Ulm, by glorying over the victory of Trafalgar, which followed immediately.

Napoleon is a little man with a hat and a sword much too big for him – as caricaturists had been drawing him for years (Isaac Cruikshank,

incidentally, was the first to caricature him, in March 1797). Napoleon's words to Mack are based on his speech to the defeated Austrians: 'I desire nothing further on the Continent; I want ships, colonies and commerce.' The loss of his fleet makes an ironic comment on his words. One of his officers bringing bad news says, '. . . Begar, if you no come back directly they vill not leave you vone boat to go over in' – over to England, that is. Britannia promises Nelson lasting fame. The following January, a drawing by George of the state carriage that carried Nelson's body to St Paul's was published as a print.

THE WIDOW WADDLE OF CHICKABIDDY LANE.
Sung by Mr GRIMALDI,

Mrs WADDLE was a widow, and she got no little gain,
She kept a tripe and trotter shop in Chickabiddy Lane;
Her next door neighbour, Tommy Tick a tallyman was he,
And he ax'd Mrs Waddle just to take a cup of tea.
with a tick a tee, tick a tee &c.

Mrs Waddle put her chintz on, and sent for Sammy Sprig,
The titwating barber, to frizify her wig; [pumps]
Tommy Tick he dress'd in pompadour, with double channel'd
And look'd when he'd his jazey on just like the Jack of Trumps
with a tick a tee, tick a tee &c.

Mrs Waddle came in time for tea, and down they sat together
They talk'd about the price of things, the fashion & the weather,
She staid to supper too, for Tommy Tick without a doubt,
Was none of them that axes you to tea and turn 'em out
with a tick a tee, tick a tee &c.

Thus, Tommy Tick, he won her hear, & they were married fast,
But all so loving were at first, 'twas thought it could not last;
They'd words, and with a large cow heel she gave him such a spe,
And he return'd the compliment with half a yard of tripe.
with a tick a tee, tick a tee &c,

She took him to the justice such cruelty to cease,
Who bound the parties over, to keep the public peace;
But Mrs Tick, one day inflam'd with max and muggy weather,
She with a joint stool broke the peace and Tommy's head together.
Spoken — there he lay, with about a dozen cowheels round him — singing, tick a tee, tick a tee &c.
London Published Oct.r 12.th 1807 by Thos. Tegg in Cheapside.

A good example of the kind of comic picture used to illustrate a popular song, the whole sheet selling for a shilling. This was sung by the great clown and comic Joseph Grimaldi.

The two figures grinning in over the counter of cow-heels are a pedlar and a chimney-sweep; the boy at the door is carrying a string of empty quart ale-pots back to a public house. George's father probably did a good part of this design. It was published by a newly-established man in the trade, Glasgow-born Thomas Tegg, opposite St Mary-le-Bow Church, for whom Isaac and George, and also Thomas Rowlandson, were to do a great deal of work. Tegg specialized in cut-price caricatures; the following year he advertised:

'A large collection (the largest in England) of new popular Humorous and Political Caricatures, by [George Moutard] Woodward, Rowlandson, Cruikshanks (sic), only one shilling each, equal to any, and superior to most, published at double the price. N.B. Please to order Tegg's New Caricatures. Noblemen, Gentlemen, etc., wishing to ornament their Billiard or other Rooms with Caricatures may be supplied one hundred per cent cheaper at Tegg's Caricature Warehouse. Merchants and Captains of Ships supplied Wholesale for Exportation.'

In the verses, a jazey is a cheap wig; max is gin.

12 October 1807

[29]

THE GOOD EFFECTS OF CARBONIC GAS!
10 December 1807

Gaslight comes to a London street in 1807, and nobody likes it except its promoter – pictured here as a sideshow performer out to make an enormous profit 'all in air, light air'. He is a German, Winzer or Winsor, of the National Light and Heat Company, who in 1807 introduced gaslight in Pall Mall and Golden Lane, Westminster. In fact, like many innovators, he went bankrupt. One investor is saying, 'I wish I had my money in my pocket.'

This caricature looks like the joint work of father and son, probably more the son. The gassed cat sliding from a roof, the bird plummeting from the sky, and the other dead, dying or retching animals and people seem the inspirations of a fifteen-year-old. It was, and is, natural for caricaturists to mock at newfangled things; George was to have plenty of other targets in the next quarter-century.

AN AFFECTING SCENE IN THE DOWNS
August 1809

George Cruikshank remembered this caricature, done in 1809 a month before he was eighteen, as the first to be published that was entirely his own work. The fat gourmand with a carbuncular nose is Alderman William Curtis, a former Lord Mayor of London, whose great fortune had been built on biscuit contracts for the navy. He was noted for his luxurious yacht, his gluttony, his illiterate speech and his devotion to the Tory government. The scene commemorated here is his visit to the fleet of more than six hundred ships assembled in July 1809 off the coast of Kent before sailing on an ill-conceived, ill-managed attempt to establish a bridgehead in the Netherlands. The weeping man in the boat is Viscount Castlereagh, who as War Secretary advocated and organized the expedition. The pretence is that he is waving a tearful farewell before the alderman sails in his yacht with the fleet – which of course he did not do. The caricature illustrates a song:

> All in the Downs the fleet was moor'd,
>   The streamers waving in the wind,
> When Castlereagh appear'd on board:
>   'Ah! where shall I my Curtis find?
> Tell me, ye jovial sailors, tell me true,
> If my fat William sails among your crew?'

> William, who high upon the poop,
>   Rock'd by the billows to and fro,
> Heard, as he supp'd his turtle-soup,

The well-known viscount's voice below.
The spoon drops greasy from his savoury hands
And quick as lightning on the deck he stands.

Cruikshank changes this a little by making the stern-deck of the yacht Curtis's galley. Behind his huge rump is a stove with a steaming cauldron of turtle soup. The spar above is garlanded with sausages, and the railing with vegetables, fish, game – and a turtle, the prime delicacy for City of London feasts. Curtis affirms his loyalty:

> 'Oh, Castlereagh, thou spotless peer!
>   My vote shall ever true remain.'

There is a pun on his wine-suffused face and the fleet's destination in the Netherlands:

> 'Though *Flushing* claim this face today,
>   Let not a paler statesman mourn.
> Though cannons roar, yet Castlereagh
>   Shall see his alderman return
> All safe and sound, tho' forc'd-meat balls should fly
> And claret still shall wet his civic eye.'

Within a few months the expedition was withdrawn. Half an army of forty thousand was lost.

BURNING THE MEMOIRS
24 April 1809

Earlier in 1809 there was a great scandal that came very near the throne, for it involved George III's favourite son, the Duke of York. The duke was an amiable, bibulous fellow and a hopeless gambler, always shamefully in debt, but he was made commander-in-chief at the king's insistence, though in two campaigns in Flanders he had proved he was no threat to Napoleon's generals. During some of the worst years of the war he maintained in great splendour a courtesan named Mary Anne Clarke. In 1809 it was revealed, after they had parted, that her lavish spending had been met partly by taking bribes from men who came to her for commissions and promotions (£400 for a lieutenant, £700 for a captain, £900 for a major). Opposition MPs led by a Colonel Gwyllym Lloyd Wardle took up the case; and the pert Mary Anne gave evidence before the House of Commons.

The senate, for gravity fam'd, may be seen
   With sides all a-shaking as gay as a lark,
As night after night to the Bar sidles in
   The dearest of dears – even dear Mrs Clarke.[86]

The duke professed to have been ignorant of what Mrs Clarke was up to, but so many MPs disbelieved him even in that corruptly well-managed House that he had to resign.

A problem remained. Mary Anne had printed 20,000 copies of her memoirs, consisting mainly of letters from the duke to his 'dearest darling' full of gossip about his parents, brothers, sisters and other exalted people. The faith of patriotic Britons had been badly enough shaken already. Ministerial threats and rewards silenced her. She handed over the letters and the books in return for £10,000 cash and £400 a year.

[32]

FRENCH GENERALS RECEIVING AN ENGLISH CHARGE
28 April 1809

The Cruikshanks were well placed to learn what was going on, for Mary Anne's publisher was in Salisbury Square, just a few paces from their house. 'Burning the Memoirs' takes a flight of fancy and shows the books being cheerfully dealt with by the Prince of Wales ('This is a fine stroke . . . John Bull will still be left in the dark, & he must pay for it at last'); the Duke of Portland, nominal prime minister ('The duchess will think me as chaste as Joseph – so much for my darling'); the printer and publisher, who also get their pay-off; and two peers who had scandals to hide. Mary Anne is walking off happily with her reward (understated).

In one of the hundreds of other caricatures on the case, Mary Anne says to the duke, 'My life and all thy darling darling love that I have with so much care treasured up, I burn, for the moderate sum of £10,000 & a small annuity, & suffer the painful restriction never more to speak thy praise . . .'

The shame that the scandal brought on the British army and nation is rubbed in by 'French Generals Receiving an English Charge' (*charge*= French for caricature). Napoleon holds an Isaac Cruikshank caricature of 1807, one of the first to hint at the scandal, 'Military Leap Frog – or Hints to Young Gentlemen'; and his words to clubfooted Talleyrand go to the heart of the matter: 'Aye, Tally, this is not the way I reward merit, by putting inexperienced boys over the heads of experienced veterans.' Talleyrand and the generals talk mockingly about the Duke of York's defeats in Flanders.

We see incidentally a good puff for five or six caricatures from the Cruikshank studio. Such things did indeed go to France. A few years earlier, when there was an interval of peace, English travellers were surprised to see Gillray caricatures adorning the walls of the French passport office at Calais.

[33]

THE RETURN TO OFFICE
1 July 1811

The larger part of the last two caricatures was probably the work of Isaac Cruikshank, with George helping; but with 'The Return to Office' we see George, soon after his father's death, and aged not yet nineteen, attaining a mature style. Here is the Duke of York, only two years after his resignation, exultantly returning to the War Office. The clue to his return is his brother George, who points the way. On coming to power as Prince Regent, George let the Tories know that he would feel more kindly towards keeping them in office, instead of bringing in his old friends the Whigs, if they restored the duke. So Spencer Perceval is sweeping Colonel Wardle aside; MPs who had voted against the duke now have stools of repentance and a bucket of whitewash, and kiss his large posterior; and a scrawny winged messenger is trumpeting (at both ends) 'He comes he comes the hero comes'. Sheridan and other Whigs are in mourning for their own patriotism: for they too were now forgiving the duke. As *The Scourge* said when it published this caricature: 'It is perfectly plain, from the whole tenor of their late conduct, that they are willing to sacrifice every feeling and every principle to the grand object of becoming the ministers of *George IV*.' (In this they failed.)

The dog urinating on Colonel Wardle has a collar saying, 'Mary Anne, late the property of the D--- but now ---' Mary Anne eventually retired to Paris with an increased pension; married off a daughter to a man named du Maurier; and became the grandmother of the artist George du Maurier . . . who was a pallbearer at George Cruikshank's funeral, sixty-seven years after the little dog was etched.

THE TREE OF CORRUPTION
1809

The Mary Anne Clarke scandal stirred up talk of reform. The man chopping at the tree is a radical MP, Sir Francis Burdett, watched by Samuel Whitbread, a reformist Whig (left, with tankard of Whitbread's), and Colonel Wardle. In the background, Sheridan the one-time denouncer of abuses stands inactive, with a small axe marked with a wine-bottle instead of with 'Justice' or 'The voice of the people'. The tree is propped by the *Morning Post,* a government-subsidized paper that valiantly supported the Duke of York and suffered a great fall in circulation – good evidence of what the public thought. But the tree still had many years to stand.

STATE MINERS
January 1811

The paunchy Alderman Curtis figures again here, among the crowd of insiders merrily shovelling up all the golden sovereigns they can get in the Treasury strongroom. Beside him is Billy's Biscuit Basket, overflowing.

Some of the other looters are, from left: in turban, Wellington's brother Lord Wellesley, saying, 'Take care of Number One'; Lord Eldon, in his long Lord Chancellor's wig, saying, 'I never care how the world wags for I've always 4,000 per annum secure in my Bags'; the prime minister, Spencer Perceval, eagerly shovelling; behind his shovel, George Canning saying to his enemy Castlereagh, 'Get out of the

way, Pat, you have no more business here than I have.'

The haste to get rich has a special point: in January 1811, the Prince of Wales, on being made Regent, was still expected to dismiss the Tories (which is why he is pictured on the wall, left, with his back turned). The centre picture on the wall, entitled 'What I Would Have if I Could', shows the prince as an infant held in leading-strings by Perceval, who says, 'Here's my pitty pincy'. On the right is a picture of mad George III as a King Lear grieving over his dead daughter, Princess Amelia.

PRINCELY PREDILECTIONS, OR ANCIENT MUSIC & MODERN DISCORD
1 April 1812 (detail)

This demonstrates how assured Cruikshank had become by the age of nineteen, less than a year after his father's death. The gross, staggering, whiskery, dishevelled Regent equals any of his later images of him. This is merely the central third of an eighteen-inch-wide folding frontispiece to the April 1812 issue of *The Scourge*. The caricature's title alludes to the Regent's remark in a public statement, justifying his abandonment of the Whigs, that he had 'no predilections to indulge, no resentments to gratify'. His predilections here are women and drink.

The man and woman immediately to each side of him are Colonel John McMahon, his private secretary and Privy Purse (often called his Privy Pimp), and McMahon's wife. The cuckold's horns on McMahon's head suggest that his wife is too intimate with the prince. But a much more important woman in the Regent's life is the one holding the leading-strings: his reigning mistress, a fifty-two-year-old grandmother, the Marchioness of Hertford. The leading-strings are fair comment – she as much as anyone decided him to keep the Tories in power, little though he liked them ('Not at all, d--n them! Not at all!!' as he says here).

The end of the leading-strings is held by a lewd Cupid wearing breeches and boots; he holds his arrow suggestively between his legs, and the tip of his wing makes a well-placed phallic hint. Behind Lady Hertford stands her marquess, sprouting cuckold's horns and looking grim. The word 'quean' used by the Scotsman (Lord Erskine, a former Lord Chancellor) means an immoral woman. It is hard to see why Cruikshank gives Lord Hertford such small horns: the prince had fallen passionately in love with Lady Hertford as long ago as 1807, and used to weep then in his tormented desire to keep his earlier great love, Mrs Fitzherbert, as well. (Mrs Fitzherbert appears here, behind the prince's left shoulder; but by 1812 he had pensioned her off with £6,000 a year.) In 1807, a man who knew all the gossip, Lord Glenbervie, wonders in his diary about the way the prince openly visits the Hertfords' town house (now the Wallace Museum): 'Lord Hertford is said to have a revenue of above £70,000. What can be the motive of his connivance . . . ?'[87] The answer may be found in the words of an old friend of the prince, Lady Bessborough. She says in a letter written shortly before the date of this caricature, 'The love of gain, it is said, pervades the whole family . . . Lady Hertford is so fond of *diamonds* that the prince's finances can hardly suffice.'[88] Soon after that, the Regent added £3,000 to Lord Hertford's income by making him Lord Chamberlain.

The Scourge, which liked Whigs no better than Tories, took a rather anarchic line on the Regent. In this same issue it attacks the Whigs for switching from praise to abuse of the Regent as soon as he dashed their hopes of office, and adds, 'Though the editor of *The Scourge* has uniformly been distinguished by his hostility to the Whigs, they have not been ashamed to furnish him with materials of attack.' But while freely abusing the Regent itself, *The Scourge* chided rival publications for doing so. In February 1812 it criticized three verse lampoons on the prince's amours. They had 'obtained an extensive circulation among the lower orders'. Such lampoons 'have a powerful influence on the lower classes; they render the names of our princes first familiar and then contemptible; they teach the peasant and the citizen to regard a court as a temple of debauchery, and the chief magistrate of the country as a drunken profligate.' All this *The Scourge* was doing too, especially in the caricatures of Cruikshank: but perhaps that was permissible because the magazine was read by the middle and upper classes. It gave its readers nearly eight pages of quoted passages from the three lampoons, tut-tutting all the way – a fine technique of virtuous thievery, still used by some journalists.

The Scourge's Tory rival, *The Satirist,* was meanwhile learning to love the Regent. It quoted a pamphlet that deplored the Whigs' new anti-Regent propaganda: 'Attempts are making to get the words "Apostate Prince" chalked on the walls during the night, and the printshops are filled with indecent caricatures . . . While they [the Whigs] were confidentially admitted at Carlton House, they made no such discoveries; now that they are excluded they see them clearly.'[89]

The Satirist also provides an interesting glimpse of another sort of opinion-management. It reports that Colonel McMahon 'has recently paid a considerable sum for the suppression of a most wicked, false, malignant, but contemptible libel, advertised for publication under the *captivating* title of "R[oya]l Stripes".' He did this with the best of motives, says *The Satirist*, 'but we trust he will on reflection see the imprudence of thus patronizing and encouraging the vile defamers of his Royal Master'. The lampoon *Royal Stripes* had merely been passed on to another publisher and issued as *The Ghost of R---l Stripes*, 'and the suppression of the former libel impudently blazoned to excite the public curiosity, and to answer the purposes of further extortion'. It ought to have been suppressed 'not by a bribe from Colonel M'M, but by a prosecution from the Attorney-General'.[90]

But so sensitive to ridicule was the Regent that suppression-by-bribe went on – although, as *The Satirist* warned, it encouraged the vile defamers. Sometimes a mere sample title-page of a lampoon or pencil sketch of a caricature was enough to extract a £50 or £100 pay-off, as the Windsor Castle archives show. McMahon and others were so co-operative that one suspects they took a cut of the money.

Caricatures were unsuppressible; but occasionally print-sellers faced direct action. *The Satirist* reports in April 1812 that a German hanger-on of the Regent, Baron Geramb, smashed a printshop window 'to demolish a caricature of a certain high personage'.

THE PRINCE OF WHALES, OR THE FISHERMAN AT ANCHOR
1 May 1812 (detail)

The Regent as whale was evidently inspired by verses of Charles Lamb, 'The Triumph of the Whale,' published a few weeks before in *The Examiner* of 15 March 1812:

> Not a fatter fish than he
> Flounders round the polar sea . . .
> Mermaids with their tails and singing
> His delighted fancy stinging . . .

But the fat and all-consuming prince had first inspired the same thought as long ago as the 1790s in a radical parody:

> O George, great Prince of WHALES,
> Thy swallow never fails,
>   Voracious prince!

> We, all your slaves, agree
> To doat on monarchy.
> Our song shall ever be
>   God save the prince.

The chief mermaid is Lady Hertford; her merman-husband has his cuckold's horns; the mermaid trying to attract the prince's attention is the ousted Mrs Fitzherbert. The whale-prince showers the Dew of Favour to the right, on to the Tories, and the Liquor of Oblivion on to the Whigs, including a hippo-Sheridan, who by this date was a sad alcoholic wreck. The swordfish bleeding golden sovereigns from the whale's side is McMahon the Privy Purse.

BONEY HATCHING A BULLETIN, OR SNUG WINTER QUARTERS!!!
December 1812

In the years 1812–15 even the Regent was upstaged as a subject by Napoleon's decline, defeat, amazing return and final exile. Cruikshank did well over a hundred caricatures on the drama. A few must suffice to show the variety of his response.

After Napoleon began retreating from Moscow with his army in October 1812, he announced that they were 'going into winter quarters'. On 27 October, before the first snows, he said, 'This weather will last eight days longer, and by that time we shall have arrived in our new position.' But on 5 December, with thousands of his men dying in the snow, he left the army in disguise and headed for Paris. This caricature was issued before the full extent of the debacle became known in London on 22 December. It makes a point that will live so long as war bulletins are made.

A RUSSIAN PEASANT LOADING A DUNG CART
1 March 1813

Caricatures had long been crossing borders. As soon as Russian morale-boosting prints arrived in London, Cruikshank began copying them, sometimes with improvements. He did nine in all for Hannah Humphrey's St James's shop. The original Russian words add to the effect. A free translation (top): *The peasant John Chiseller* – 'Halt, M'sieu, not so fast! Here you see men and Russians.' (Bottom): 'Look, we've got carts ready to load you up and carry you off. Now, M'sieu! Off you go!' The Russians became the instant heroes of the anti-Napoleonic world, for they promised an end to the war at last. But Napoleon had a while to go yet.

COMPARATIVE ANATOMY,
OR BONE-YS NEW CONSCRIPTS FILLING UP THE SKELETONS
OF THE OLD REGIMENTS
1 November 1813

In the autumn of 1813 a bulletin of Napoleon reached England that was translated to say he had a 'transcendent design of reinforcing the skeletons of all his old soldiers' (and in fact he did make another big levy of young conscripts that winter). With a mameluke beside him, poor Napoleon, equipped with a bigger hat and sword than ever, now that his fortunes are sinking, directs the rebuilding of his army. The standard-bearer adds to the boney joke.

LA CHEF DE LA GRANDE NATION DANS UNE TRISTE POSITION

early 1814

Here is evidence of the impact Cruikshank had made by the age of twenty-one. It is one of at least seven copies of his caricatures made for distribution in France as propaganda between late 1813 and 1815. They were probably made in London and shipped over. Their effect is likely to have been all the sharper because until then the French had not been seeing anything that mocked their emperor: his police suppressed all critical caricatures.

The Cruikshank original, published December 1813, was entitled 'The HEAD of the Great Nation in a Queer Situation!' Napoleon is beset by (from left to right) Wellington, Francis I of Austria, Bernadotte of Sweden, Alexander of Russia, and a Netherlander. The French is a flavourless translation. Wellington says, 'Take a good aim at the *head*, gentlemen, & we shall soon settle the business.' Bernadotte (betrayer of Napoleon): 'By gar we shall mak de head look like de plomb pudding.' Alexander: 'I'll rattle a few snowballs at his cranium.'

[43]

A GRAND MANOEUVRE! OR THE ROGUE'S MARCH TO THE ISLAND OF ELBA
13 April 1814

The news that Napoleon had agreed to abdicate and go to Elba reached London on 9 April 1814, and Cruikshank's comment was published four days later. Napoleon's stripped insignia and broken sword lie on the ground and he is being treated like a disgraced officer, with his spurs reversed and his coat back-to-front. He weeps and he is emaciated (in fact he was overweight). His baby son announces, 'By gar Papa I have made von *grand manoeuvre* in your pocket!!' – this phrase, here and in the title, being a sardonic allusion to some of the great army movements by which Napoleon had formerly gained his victories.

A devil is to convey Napoleon to Elba, where a gallows awaits him. A fiddler-devil dances on his head. The crowd of sudden enthusiasts for the restoration of the Bourbons are pelting him with the sort of nasty rubbish that was hurled in England at a man in the pillory. A fifer is playing and singing:

> He was whipped and he was drummed,
> He was drummed out of the regiment.
> If ever he is a soldier again
> The devil may be his sergeant.

But the caricature does not ask us to admire the people crying '*A bas le tyran . . . Vive Louis XVIII*'; and the clubfooted Talleyrand, the adroit turncoat survivor, looks too gloatingly pleased.

[44]

LITTLE BONEY GONE TO POT

12 May 1814

Napoleon reached Elba on 4 May 1814, and Cruikshank had this on sale the following week. The Imperial Throne is a huge chamberpot, which makes Napoleon tinier than ever. He is a sick man: he has an enema bag under his left arm, medicine bottles beside him, a jar of brimstone for the itch. His cannon is a mock-up from an old boot.

PREPARING FOR WAR

1 June 1815 (detail)

Within ten months Napoleon was back in France, and Louis found that he was not a beloved king. Nor was Britain altogether enthusiastic about going to war again to put him back on his shaky throne. Less than three weeks before the Battle of Waterloo, this is how Cruikshank saw things. The Regent, lolling beneath a canopy decorated with naked women, grapes, wineglasses and a bottle, says, 'Why, this looks like war! Order me a brilliant fete, send me a myriad of cooks & scullions, say to me no more of Civil Lists & deserted wives but of luxurious mistresses & Bacchanalian orgies [the last seven words are painted over]. To it pell mell – my soul is eager for the fierce encounter – what – are my whiskers easier than they were?' McMahon and a coiffeur barber him and a stay-maker says, 'I think these will be the best stays your Highness has had yet.'

The British bull, 'sacred to the Bourbon cause,' says, '. . . Have I bled for so many years in your service and will you now take my life?' He is about to be roasted; Liverpool, the prime minister, is sharpening a knife; Castlereagh gives him a lecture: '. . . War, war, interminable war, I say. Down with the regicide, no quarter to the usurper . . . All I ask is that I may live to preach your funeral sermon.' The sacks with gaping

mouths are marked 'For subsidies' – that is, for Britain's allies, yet again. The bull carries an endless list of taxes: '. . . windows dogs houses servants clerks shopmen carts hair-powder horses . . .'

Across the channel, the fat, indolent, gouty, sixty-year-old Louis XVIII, supported on a Talleyrand-donkey and a crutch, advances to battle with medicine phials and a roll of flannel as mock guns. Further off, Blucher is sharpening his sword. Far to the right, in a section not reproduced here, Napoleon and his army are arriving.

To some extent this is an unfair picture of the Regent: he was an enthusiast for the war both in 1813–14 and at the time of Waterloo. He took court flattery literally and believed that his 'wise counsels' had been the deciding factor. When he heard in April 1814 that the allies had entered Paris, he wrote to Queen Charlotte: 'I trust my dearest mother that you will think that I have fulfilled and done my duty at last, and perhaps I may be vain enough to hope that you may feel a little proud of *your son*.'[91] In later years he believed (with the aid of laudanum) that he had led a victorious charge at Waterloo. Wellington is reported to have said to him: 'I have heard you, sir, say so before, but I did not witness this marvellous charge.'[92]

[46]

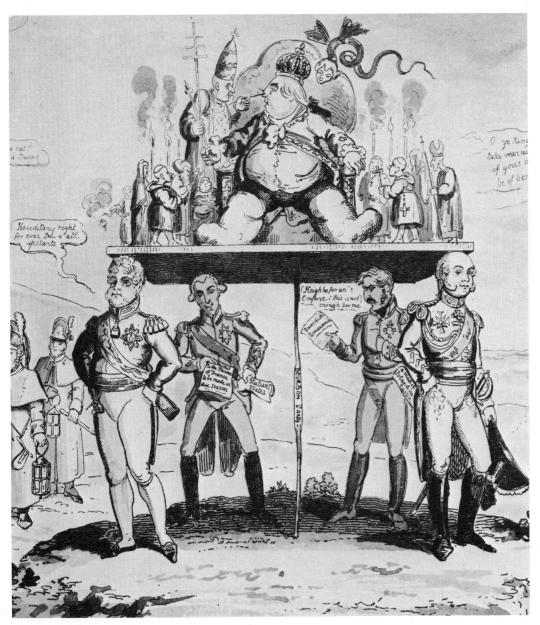

THE STATE OF POLITICKS AT THE CLOSE OF THE YEAR 1815,
1 December 1815 (detail)

After Waterloo, the re-restored Louis XVIII was more than ever the creation of others. The 'Bourbon party' is a mere frail stick and his true supporters are the Regent, the Emperor of Austria, King Frederick William of Prussia and Alexander I of Russia. The Regent, bottle in hand, corkscrew at belt, and decorated with bottles and naked women, says, 'Hereditary right for ever. D--n all up-starts.' The Austrian emperor has got back his Italian states and is thinking of claiming the French throne (after all, he had married his daughter to Napoleon when that seemed best in the power game). The Prussian king has enlarged his realm but is not satisfied. Alexander has Poland in his pocket. Up above, Louis is firmly controlled by the Pope.

In the portions of this caricature not reproduced here, Frenchmen with two faces are shouting 'Vive le Roi . . . Vive l'Empereur!' and Ferdinand VII of Spain, wearing a blindfold labelled Bigotry and with death warrants in his pocket, has a hook in his nose like Louis and is led along by a friar. *The Scourge*, in the issue in which this appeared, says, 'Priests and the devil rule in Spain – priests and old women, with the aid and co-operation of the allies, in France.' Britain 'comes in only for the *honour*, and even for that she *pays dearly enough*'.

JOHN BULL
IN THE COUNCIL CHAMBER
1 July 1813 (detail)

The Regent's mother, Queen Charlotte, had been pictured for many years as avaricious and ill-natured. This detail from a nineteen-inch-wide *Scourge* caricature of July 1813 shows that the confinement of her husband at Windsor Castle did not bring her more sympathetic treatment. Her straddle-legged pose would have been thought shockingly improper for a humble woman, let alone a queen. The grotesque courtiers are serving her with snuff, of which she was so fond that she was nicknamed Old Snuffy. The imps on the left are dancing in with more supplies.

The Queen's foot is planted on a plump footstool labelled 'Hastings Diamonds', an allusion to the precious gifts that reached the queen from India in 1786 at a time when Warren Hastings was under investigation for his ruthless empire-building and profiteering. Jewels were her passion; a second nickname was Queen of Diamonds; when she died in 1818 it was estimated by John Wilson Croker – no critic, but a loyal Tory – that her personal collection was worth £200,000, a vast fortune then.

In the full caricature the Regent may be seen as a baby in a cradle, a way of saying that he is managed by his ministers and his mother. She is demanding full details of a secret inquiry into the varied amours of the Regent's wife, Princess Caroline.

COSTUME OF A GROOM OF THE STOLE:
LORD P-T--SH-M
November 1813

An early style-setter for the dandies who were to flourish after the war: Lord Petersham, a Lord of the Bedchamber to George III and later to George IV. An article accompanying this study in *The Meteor* says there are various ways to commend oneself to the Regent, but Petersham's is the best. 'Adultery is a pleasing venality – a certain recommendation of a peer at Court... Seduction, hard drinking, boxing, or taking up with a cast-off mistress, have each their recommendative good qualities... But, my lord, dress – dress, in everything complete, is the *sine qua non* of modern excellence; and without the study of which a lord would... be degraded into the semblance of A MAN!... But look, my lord, look with complacency on the accompanying sketch... Does it resemble in any one feature a human being?... Does it not rather resemble a young bear, with... his body screwed up in a tight pair of stays, his shoulders swelled out with stuffing in rising tufts, and his head dipping out of a bolster of folded cambric...?'

In a time of social extremes and conspicuous display, fashions blatantly unsuited to everyday work are generally in demand to distinguish a privileged person from ordinary mortals – a point made by *The Meteor*. The Regent's obsession with clothes helped to push things further; and there was also something of a last-fling mood as unrest threatened the age of rich sinecures and arrogant spending. Even for that time, Petersham was something special. He was said to have a snuff-box for each day of the year. Captain Rees Gronow says in his memoirs that when someone admired one of Petersham's Sèvres snuffboxes, 'I heard him say in his lisping way – Yes, it is a nice summer box, but would not do for winter wear.'[93]

A LEVEE DAY
1 April 1814

The Regent is tormented by the vapours, the dropsy and the gout (his swollen foot goaded by fiends closely resembles a Gillray of 1799, 'The Gout'). He is in no mood to respond to any of the demands on his attention at his levee.

On left, the Home Secretary, Lord Sidmouth, wants to report on a stock exchange coup of February 1814 in which some smart operators made more than £10,000 by spreading a false report of Napoleon's death (Sidmouth displays two of Cruikshank's caricatures on the affair). Next is the Prime Minister, Lord Liverpool, with important news: 'Dispatches from Lord Wellington. The defeat of Soult!! Bordeaux in our possession!!! Buonaparte defeated by Blucher!!!' Haughty Lady Hertford, who was a mother as well as a mistress to the Regent, presses him: 'Come deary, take a little of my turtle soup.' A goblin labelled Dropsy comes between the soup and the royal mouth, holding up a glass and singing an old catch, 'Punch cures the gout, the colic & the phthisic.' Under the Regent's foot is a copy of *The Meteor* (the monthly for which this caricature was done) displaying an earlier Cruikshank; and at the Regent's left hand is a further piece of Cruikshank self-advertisement: another *Meteor* with a caricature of the man who is holding it, the Earl of Yarmouth.

Next come two important people in the Regent's life: his tailor, with instructions for new coats and breeches and with unpaid bills in his pocket; and his wigmaker, bearing a wig 'which I confidently present as the best in christendom'. This last phrase suggests that Cruikshank, like other caricaturists, looked to the satirical verses of Thomas Moore

for ideas. In a collection then on sale, *Intercepted Letters or the Twopenny Post-Bag*, he calls the Regent 'The best-wigg'd prince in christendom'.

Last in the queue is the Recorder of London, John Silvester, a notoriously severe judge, holding a black bag full of death warrants 'for stealing cheeses . . . for stealing bread . . . for stealing meat'. He says, 'I must wait till these weighty matters are dealt with.' The Regent was shamefully dilatory in dealing with death warrants, whether through squeamishness or sloth: more likely the latter, for at his death his successor, William IV, found more than forty-eight thousand documents of all kinds awaiting signature.

Beside the Regent's seething head perches his devoted Irish secretary McMahon, saying, 'Oh! by the powers my honey, you must not go & leave all these good things behind you.' And indeed he had been very ill. The month before Cruikshank drew this in March 1814, the memoirist Charles Greville recorded in his journal, 'The Regent was very near dying in consequence of a disgraceful debauch.' He liked a great range of drinks. In 1811 Lord Glenbervie records that 'his favourite dram at present' is a flavoured concoction called Eau de Garuche, 'excessively strong and hot', and at one dinner the Regent has drunk 'at least three bottles of wine, besides maraschino punch and the Eau de Garuche'. With all this and what he himself called 'immense quantities' of laudanum, he often got into a bad mental state. When he was very ill in 1811, says Lady Bessborough, his brother the Duke of Cumberland was saying everywhere that his illness 'was *higher* than the foot' – which needed no explaining when his father had just been declared mad.[94]

AN EXCURSION TO R----- HALL
1 October 1812

The Hertfords' town house in Manchester Square became a second home for the Regent. When they went to the country he felt abandoned and sorry for himself. One of his secretaries, Benjamin Bloomfield, writes to Lord Hertford in 1807 to say that the prince is in 'the greatest agony' about some family trouble, and quotes him as saying, 'If Lord and Lady Hertford were but here, the only persons to whom I can talk and confide! What is now to become of me, of wretched me?' Three days later they are hurrying back to London from Ragley, Warwickshire (still the Hertford country house) and the prince says, 'Thank God they are coming!... Oh, this is a relief for poor me.'[95]

Sometimes the prince made the trip to Ragley. Here Cruikshank commemorates such an occasion. The golden-horned Lord Hertford leads the procession as it nears his great estate. He rides a donkey and holds his Lord Chamberlain's stick erect. The postilion is a booted half-naked blindfold Cupid in a jockey cap. The carriage is driven by a devil. His friend is the Hertfords' dissolute son, the redhaired Earl of Yarmouth. The following year *The Scourge* printed some savage verses about him (though not of course actually naming him):

> The envy of each younger brother,
> The willing pander to his mother.
> To lie, seduce and drink for ever,
> In cheating use his best endeavour,
> And once a week on subject pretty
> Indite and sing a bawdy ditty,
> Were all his serious labours, since

No others satisfy a prince...
Since the time of Charles the Second
No pimp could be his equal reckoned...[96]

It may be thought fitting that he was the prince's Vice-Chamberlain.

'We have had a glorious ride, my love,' says the enormously full-figured marchioness. 'It is worth *half a crown*.' The prince regrets he has not half a crown to give her (he is married). McMahon is their footman. The carriage is the 'old yellow chariot' in which the prince used to drive (with the top up and blinds drawn) from Carlton House to Manchester Square; and which Thomas Moore put into his 'Extracts from the Diary of a Politician':

> Through M-nch-st-r Square took a canter just now –
> Met the *old yellow chariot* and made a low bow.
> This I did of course thinking 'twas loyal and civil,
> But got such a look – oh, 'twas black as the devil!

For the prince wished to be *incog*. The politician makes a memo:

> When next by the old yellow chariot I ride,
> To remember there *is* nothing princely inside.[97]

Next in the procession comes Sheridan as a tattered harlequin, on a donkey with a wine-barrel for saddle. Last of all is a wagon labelled: 'For Yarmouth. Second-hand pieces from Wales' – meaning girls whom Yarmouth is taking over from the prince. Beside the road, in an asylum for older cast-offs, Mrs Fitzherbert laments, '...He has forgot his poor F.'

[51]

ALL THE WORLD'S IN PARIS
1 February 1815

A star of the theatre whose fame still lives: Joseph Grimaldi (1779–1837), comedian, singer and clown, in whose honour a clown is still known as a joey. His coat with its embroidery and huge cuffs and collar is related to the one worn by a dandy in 'Monstrosities of 1816'. The print illustrates a song 'sung with great applause by Mr Grimaldi in the popular pantomime of ''Harlequin Whittington''', about the rush of tourists to Paris after the peace of 1814:

Age throws off his winter cough,
    Gout forgets his flannel;
Small and great at Dover wait
    To cross the British Channel . . .

Players, peers and auctioneers,
    Parsons, undertakers,
Modish airs from Wapping Stairs,
    Wit from Norton Falgate,
Bagatelle from Clerkenwell
    And elegance from Aldgate.

London now is out of town;
    Who in England tarries?
Who can bear to linger there
    When all the world's in Paris?

. . . Thus we dance through giddy France
    And when we find the fun done,
The piper pay, and march away
    With empty purse to London.

[52]

SCENE IN THE COMIC OPERA OF THE LORD OF THE MANOR:
SONG, MOLL FLAGGON, SUNG BY MR LISTON
20 January 1815

Stagestruck as he was, Cruikshank had the good luck to grow up in a time of great performers, if not of great playwrights. Here is one of his favourites in action. The dancing, pipe-smoking man in drag is the comedian John Liston (?1776–1846), playing the part of Moll Flaggon in a revival of 'Gentleman John' Burgoyne's comedy *The Lord of the Manor* (1781). In that year, the song that Moll Flaggon sings must have been a welcome antidote to disastrous news from America:

Come, my soul,
  Post the cole, [*hand over money*]
I must beg or borrow.
  Fill the can,
  You're my man,
'Tis all the same tomorrow.

Sing and quaff,
Dance and laugh,
A fig for care or sorrow.
  Kiss and drink
  But never think:
'Tis all the same tomorrow.

MONSTROSITIES OF 1816: SCENE, HYDE PARK

12 March 1816

The full comicality of odd fashions is lost with the passing of years, for almost everything becomes indistinguishably quaint. But a close look at Regency clothes shows that things were odder than usual, not to say queer. The women (continuing the liberation that had begun in the 1790s) exposed a great deal of themselves, and forgot they had waists. The men choked themselves, became wasp-waisted and full-hipped, and concealed their hitherto well-displayed legs in many sorts of transitional trousers.

Cruikshank's view of the fashionables in one of the London parks is scarcely exaggerated. The skirts of 1816 are shockingly short. Seldom had men been able to delight publicly in so much female leg (though the hoop skirts of the early eighteenth century permitted their moments). Women's undress had been worrying the censorious for some years. In 1812 a book called *Metropolitan Grievances* says, 'Young rakes, but more particularly veteran debauchees . . . eye with rapture . . . the transparent drapery of luxurious nakedness . . . These thinly clad damsels you will see perambulating the fashionable streets, the parks and Kensington Gardens, exposing with other parts of the person, *beautiful ruby* arms, and *raspberry-jam* coloured elbows . . .'[98] *The Scourge* talks of 'muslin damped to assimilate more easily with their lovely limbs, arms exposed to the very pits . . . cases [boned brassières] after the eastern mode to prop up and show to advantage the bosom'. But the men 'seem to think they cannot cover themselves too much'. Their necks are 'wrapped round with more yards of muslin than would make a belle a robe'.[99]

With the end of the war, everything French was desirable again, and the British seized on Paris styles and perhaps overdid them. The strange stoop of the women, which aided their frontal display, was from France: a satirical book illustrated by Cruikshank, *Fashion*, speaks of fashionable Englishwomen 'Arriv'd from abroad with *les airs de Paris*/With stoop of fair shoulder.'[100] But another wicked influence was the Regent's court. A satirical monthly, *The Busy Body*, says: 'This custom of removing all restraints and cloaks from nature has been adopted out of compliment to the Prince Regent, whose eyes, I believe, are pretty much accustomed to sin'; his twenty-year-old daughter Princess Charlotte, it says, 'has adopted a costume, the wearer of which, in lower life, would stand a very excellent chance of being hissed out of the theatres and hooted through the streets.'[101]

This was the year in which trousers, which not long before had been a dubious, democratic, levelling French fashion, became acceptable in London for evening as well as day wear. In the park parade they became a means of self-expression. The man lifting his hat almost looks as if he is wearing skirts. The man on the right has trousers tied with ribbons above high-heeled boots. His arm-in-arm companion might almost be taken for a woman: his ground-length coat heavily trimmed with fur was perhaps inspired by Russian officers' winter wear. Russians had been heroes since 1812; and the full trousers seen here were called cossacks.

The perversity of the male silhouette aroused comments. The book *Fashion* talks of bluestocking women with 'gentlemanlike deportment . . . the short crop . . . and masculine ensemble', and goes on: 'The brief waist pinched in at the bottom, pigeon tail, large hips, tight stays and padded bosom of the young lisping male tribe seem to imitate the softer sex.'[102]

It was a bad time for those who hated change, and especially for crusty scholars such as Francis Douce of the British Museum, who wrote in his journal: 'The bucks of the present time, 1814–15, wear their coats so tight that it is almost impossible to get a tailor to make you a garment that does not put you to the torture.'[103]

THE BLESSINGS OF PEACE OR THE CURSE OF THE CORN BILL

3 March 1815

Peace made continental grain available once more, a disturbing prospect for English landowners, who had done well through the war.

> Safe in their barns, these Sabine tillers sent
> Their brethren out to battle – why? – for rent!
> Year after year they voted cent per cent,
> Blood, sweat and tear-wrung millions – why? for rent!
> They roar'd, they dined, they drank, they swore they meant
> To die for England – why then live? – for rent!
> The peace has made one general malcontent
> Of these high-market patriots; war was rent!

So said Byron in 'The Age of Bronze'; and so thought hundreds of thousands of people who petitioned parliament early in 1815 when the government brought in a Bill requiring that any imported grain cheaper than eighty shillings a bushel should pay duty. Cruikshank timed this caricature for the day before a mass meeting in London on 4 March 1815 to petition against the Bill, and it is reasonable to assume that it helped to inspire some of the 40,571 signatures collected that day . . . in vain.

If the poor cannot afford the high price, says one gentleman, rejecting fifty-shilling French wheat, 'Why, they must starve, we love money too well . . .' A sturdy John Bull, standing with his sorrowing family in front of a storehouse of eighty-shilling sacks, says: 'No, no, masters, I'll not starve but quit my native country . . .' And indeed the great nineteenth-century emigration soon began.

[56]

ECONOMICAL HUMBUG OF 1816, OR SAVING AT THE SPIGOT & LETTING OUT AT THE BUNGHOLE

28 April 1816

It is puzzling to John Bull that although the Chancellor of the Exchequer, Nicholas Vansittart, has 'thrown away the great *war* spigot' and 'substituted a small *peace* one', his taxes seem to be swallowed up as fast as ever. The Regent provides the answer: 'Come, my friends, make haste & fill your buckets whilst Van is keeping noisy Johnny quiet with fine speeches & promises of economy, which I am determined not to practise . . .' In the midst of an economic crisis, the opposition had begun attacking extravagance as soon as parliament met in February 1816. Liverpool, Castlereagh and Vansittart wrote to the Regent asking him to promise to abandon 'all new expenses for additions or alterations at Brighton or elsewhere'. If he were not seen to economize, they said, 'it will be represented most unjustly as indicating an insensibility on the part of your Royal Highness and of your Ministers to the suffering & deprivations of others.'[104] The Regent, perhaps encouraged by that

tactful 'most unjustly', did not retrench, although widespread distress was sharpening the cry for radical reform, and he was more than £500,000 in debt. One small example of his defiance of his ministers' plea: the following year he spent £5,553 on a chandelier for Brighton Pavilion – or a year's wages for more than two hundred labourers.

The man with the bucket marked 'For cottages and pavillons' is John Nash, a great inciter of royal spending, who had just finished building The Cottage at Windsor – a thatched, mock-gothic pleasure-house of which one MP said, 'The Prince Regent expends as great a sum for a thatched cottage as another monarch would on a palace.'

The man collecting '60,000 for fun' is Prince Leopold, the subject of the next caricature, who was granted that annual sum for marrying the Regent's daughter.

A BRIGHTON HOT BATH, OR PREPARATIONS FOR THE WEDDING!! April 1816

No native Briton was officially admissible to marry the then heir to the throne, the Regent's only legitimate child, twenty-year-old Princess Charlotte. Foreign suitors were resented by the public as impoverished princelings on the make. The peace celebrations of 1814 brought, among others, Prince Leopold of Saxe-Coburg-Gotha:

> Being a youth of comely size
> He catched our r---l miss's eyes;
> She sigh'd, 'He is a handsome figure,
> I would not wish a husband bigger.'

So said a lampoon, *Wooing!! and Cooing!! – The R---l Courtship,* published by one of Cruikshank's caricature outlets, John Fairburn. In the spring of 1816, when the wedding was delayed on account of Leopold's ill-health there was some unpleasant talk, and another of Cruikshank's publishers, James Johnston, printed some verses about an alleged clandestine affair of Leopold's from which 'some ills' resulted:

> Some swore his H[ighne]ss was grown coy,
> Others threw out, he was infected.

As usual, a caricature goes much further. Leopold is in the tub getting one of the ancient treatments for venereal disease, sweating. A glimpse of a statue of Mercury announces another treatment, and there is an array of potions . . . and little phallic hints. Queen Charlotte pours in hot water, Lord Chancellor Eldon rubs with his long wig, the Regent recollects that he was 'served this way myself some twenty years ago'.

Princess Charlotte's death in childbirth the following year robbed Leopold of his future as prince consort, but he kept £50,000 a year for life and became Leopold I of the Belgians and Queen Victoria's uncle.

MISS MARY & HER LOVING COUSIN! OR SINGLE GLOUCESTER PREFERRED TO GERMAN SAUSAGE!!!
June 1816

George III and Queen Charlotte had perversely kept their daughters unmarried into middle age. In July 1816, at the age of forty, Princess Mary dared to defy her mother and marry her cousin, the Duke of Gloucester, known as Silly Billy or Slice of Single Gloucester. Although he was the son of one of George III's brothers, he had never been granted the title Royal Highness because his mother was a commoner; worse, she was the illegitimate daughter of Sir Edward Walpole by a girl of humble birth. In Queen Charlotte's eyes, that ruled him out as a son-in-law. The queen, being from the tiny German principality of Mecklenburgh-Strelitz, had great royal pride. Her son William used to describe how, when Napoleon married the Austrian emperor's daughter in 1810, the queen was so outraged that she exclaimed between large doses of snuff, 'My Gott! My Gott! What will this come to? The oldest house in Europe married to an emperor of yesterday! My Gott! My Gott! married to *nothing* – he has no blood in his veins.'[105]

Another lampoon published by Fairburn, *Fair! Fat! and Forty! – More R---l Coupling!!*, says the cousins 'had lov'd for years', and asks, 'Why, when the K--g had given consent/Could not old *Plug-nose* be content?' It puts the queen's view like this:

Der Jarman preed shoult not be mixt
Vith common stock, dat she vas fix'd.

The song the fond couple sing commends them for not marrying Germans. One set of phallic symbols is on the side table: 'German sausages to be sent back again untasted'; another one lies on the floor – a field marshal's baton awarded by the Regent 'for kissing his sister'. 'Farmer George's Daughter Polly', another Cruikshank caricature, has McMahon delivering the baton and saying: 'Please, sir, my master has sent you this *churning stick* as you are so kind as to work in his sister's *buttery.*'

[59]

SALUTING THE R----T'S BOMB, UNCOVERED ON HIS BIRTHDAY
August 12th 1816

This caricature, one of Cruikshank's first jobs for the radical publisher William Hone, was inspired by the unveiling on Horse Guards Parade, on the Regent's fifty-fourth birthday, of an ornate mortar presented to him by the Spanish Cortes. The mortar (still on view) was called a bomb – pronounced bum. A lampoon published by Fairburn has the Regent thinking what show he can put on to dazzle John Bull:

> Yes: since I find to *show my face*
> But brings groans, hisses and disgrace,
> To strike my subject Bull quite dumb
> I'faith I will *expose my Bomb*.

The words that Cruikshank gives the various worshippers of the Bomb are adapted from verses written by William Hone for a broadside.

The hags are (left to right) Lady Hertford, aged fifty-six, the reigning mistress; Maria Fitzherbert, sixty, his greatest love, whom he married illegally in 1785; and Lady Jersey, sixty-three, his mistress in the 1790s. (The threesome were topical because they had recently all turned up, embarrassingly, at a ball attended by the Regent.) Old Bags is Lord Eldon, Lord Chancellor, carrying mace and Woolsack. Other worshippers are Nicholas Vansittart, Chancellor of the Exchequer; William Pole-Tylney-Long-Wellesley, famous for having married an heiress who had rejected the Regent's brother William; Castlereagh (who has adopted trousers); and George Rose, who managed the secret rewards that kept MPs loyal and selected newspapers friendly.

In this print, the full names were written in after it left the shop.

[60]

THE ROYAL SHAMBLES
OR THE PROGRESS OF LEGITIMACY & RE-ESTABLISHMENT OF RELIGION
AND SOCIAL ORDER–!!!–!!!
August 1816 (detail)

This is only the lefthand two-thirds of the largest and most crowded caricature that Cruikshank made – twenty-one inches wide and selling for four shillings. He was on holiday at Margate when he etched it for William Hone, and he appears to have given it a great deal of loving labour. Hone and Cruikshank fervently agreed in disliking the Holy Alliance.

In the foreground, Louis XVIII moves in procession from right to left, mounted on a cannon marked Jure Divino and led by Wellington, who says, 'Hold fast & never fear – but if you let go my sword you'll fall *head foremost*.' Beneath the spiked boots of the marchers and the spiked wheels of the cannon lie the dead and dying bodies of republicans, some wearing the revolutionary *bonnet rouge*. Monks leading the procession are zealously bashing the heads of two men. Louis is accompanied by the Austrian emperor, the Prussian king, the Tsar –

and John Bull, who gets sprayed with holy water and is the only one who looks unhappy.

Louis's cry of 'Petition me no petitions', and the fainting mother of two children behind him, refer to an event of the month before. The wife of Jacques Pleignier, a man implicated in a conspiracy against Louis, pleaded for his life and was spurned. And the very different procession moving from left to right in the background represents, with some exaggeration, the sequel: Pleignier and two others had their right hands chopped off, and then were decapitated.

The guillotine in the background, carefully placed above Louis's head, is a reminder of the fate suffered by his brother Louis XVI twenty-three years before. Louis XVIII was anxious not to depart 'head foremost', and the following month he dissolved a chamber in which awkward ultra-royalists had a majority.

INCONVENIENCES OF A CROWDED DRAWING-ROOM

6 May 1818

The scene is Buckingham House (now Palace) during one of the last formal receptions, known as drawing-rooms, given by Queen Charlotte before her death in 1818. There was 'an immense crowd . . . much confusion', says Captain Gronow in his memoirs. 'Everyone wished to get first into the presence of royalty, much rushing and squeezing took place, loud shrieks were heard and several ladies fainted.'[106] The men in their goldlaced court dress, with eighteenth-century bagwigs and *chapeau bras*, or in dress uniforms, and the ladies in their wide-hipped dresses, make for Cruikshank a delightful grotesque chaos. The climax is the doorway encounter, with the entire mass of the woman bearing down through the point of one toe into the man's swollen gouty foot.

Above may be seen the lower part of a portrait of the queen enthroned; and of the Regent as a hussar.

LIBERTY SUSPENDED!–WITH THE BULWARK OF THE CONSTITUTION!

March 1817

For twenty years the war had served as an excuse for putting off reform. But now the Liverpool-Castlereagh government was as determined as ever to yield nothing. Economic distress and the contrasting sight of royal and noble squandering stimulated the growth of reform movements. A few desperate plots were stimulated too, with the help of agents-provocateurs. In December 1816 a tiny group, the Spenceans, who had a vision of communal wealth-sharing, caused panic in London by rampaging away from a meeting in Spa Fields, Clerkenwell, seizing a few guns and making a doomed foray towards the Tower. In January the Regent, returning from Parliament, was hissed as usual; and something (alleged by the government to be a bullet) broke a pane of his carriage. The Home Secretary, Lord Sidmouth, laid before Parliament a mass of papers alleging a revolutionary plot.

This caricature comments on what swiftly followed: the passage of Bills to suspend habeas corpus, further restrict the press, and severely limit political activity. Castlereagh, demonstrating how liberty has been 'suspended', says, 'It is better to do this than *stand prostrate . . .*' The italicized words are from one of the inept speeches for which he was noted. Beside him the Lord Chancellor holds a bag of 'evidence against Liberty': 'Spenceans' plan – Spa Fields plot – an old stocking full of gunpowder – 3 or 4 rusty firearms . . .' The bag has pig's feet: a pig in a poke. On the left the Archbishop of Canterbury is intoning prayers of thanksgiving for the Regent's escape from 'the madness of the people' – the actual phrase used.

The platform on which all this goes on is a stripped-down version of the hand-operated press then generally in use: a symbol of liberty that was to be much displayed in the next few years. All round is an approving audience of guardsmen and plump sinecurists.

[63]

THE HOMBOURG WALTZ, WITH CHARACTERISTIC SKETCHES OF FAMILY DANCING!

4 May 1818

The waltz was seen as a wanton dance, putting couples into much too intimate contact.

> Hoops are *no more*, and petticoats *not much*;
> Morals and minuets, virtue and her stays,
> And tell-tale powder – all have had their days.
> Round all the confines of the yielded waist,

The strangest hand may wander undisplaced;
> The lady's in return may grasp as much
> As princely paunches offer to her touch.
> Pleased round the chalky floor how well they trip,
> One hand reposing on the royal hip.

So wrote Byron in The Waltz in 1813.

In this caricature of May 1818, the lascivious dance is made a sexual metaphor. The central figures are Princess Elizabeth, another of George III's unhappy daughters, aged forty-eight, and the Prince of Hesse-Homburg, who had just married – in defiance, again, of Queen Charlotte. Their dialogue alludes to her past:

Prince: You do it very easy my love ! ! ! Is dis de first time you dance dis valtz?
Princess: First time 'pon honour but 'tis a delightful dance and I knew we should soon get into it.

There are many reasons for believing that satirists and others had been justified in their suggestions for thirty years past that Princess Elizabeth, a warm-natured girl, had had several children. One of her lovers, in the 1780s, is said to have been a palace barber named Stone. A Fairburn lampoon of 1818 (when, after Princess Charlotte's death, a number of George III's ageing children became eager to beget heirs) has the Regent say of Elizabeth:

> She hunting for the heir must go;
> She's used enough to hair, you know.
> Witness the Barber, who, they say,
> To dress her *wig* came ev'ry day;
> With him she had as pretty sport
> As ever had been known at C---t.
> *Two heirs*, 'tis known, they got together,
> Hunting the hair in May-day weather;
> Till Friz gave tongue, the foolish lad!
> And then we swore the rogue was *mad*.
> . . . So still he in a madhouse lies
> And for his *boys* and *Betsy* sighs.[107]

This sending of the lover to a madhouse is mentioned in print as early as 1788. The man's name is hinted at more than once in 1818 by the printseller J. L. Marks, who describes caricatures on the subject as 'Printed from Stone!' One of these shows some children labelled 'Bett's Chickens' being got out of the way while Queen Charlotte assures the angry husband, 'I tell you my daughter was a *maid* . . . so let's have none of your *humbugs*!'

The Fairburn lampoon's description of Elizabeth cruelly matches Cruikshank's picture:

> Pray, did you ever see, my masters,
> A round of beef that mov'd on castors?
> So Betsy mov'd, so plump, so squab,
> So fitted for a *melting job*.

Behind the pillar, the Regent talks about the partner he long ago got rid of, Caroline, and alludes to her loose reputation before marriage ('I found she had been dancing before'). Facing him, the future William IV, whom several women had rejected because he was so graceless, says, 'D....d hard lines that I can't get a partner'.

The Duke of York, balder and fatter than in 1811, marches along (past a 'list of discarded Clarkes'), saying to the musicians, 'Play Paddy *Carey* [a dance tune] & be d----d to you' – meaning that he prefers his mistress, Mrs Carey, successor to Mary Anne Clarke, to any wife. Two of the men on the right are mentioned sarcastically in Byron's Waltz:

> Some potentate – or royal or serene –
> With Kent's gay grace, or sapient Gloster's mien,
> Leads forth the ready dame . . .

Gloucester is the splayfooted one with his Mary. The bald-headed non-dancer is the Duke of Kent – not yet married, but at fifty-one he had cast aside his mistress after twenty-seven years, and then:

> To couple soon is his intent
> With C[obur]g's sister, tallyho!
> And then to *hunt the heir* they'll go.

A year later he became the father of the heir that mattered: Victoria.

On the right sits old Queen Charlotte, mother of the princes and princesses, saying, 'This is rather late in the evening to begin waltzing, my little dears' (the fault was hers). The man dancing outside the door is Ernest, Duke of Cumberland. The queen refused to receive at court his German bride, who had notoriously misbehaved herself. The queen says, 'He shan't bring his partner to dance in my room'.

THE PICCADILLY NUISANCE, DEDICATED TO THE WORTHY ACTING MAGISTRATES OF THE DISTRICT
29 December 1818

Hatchett's Hotel in Piccadilly was a terminus for stagecoaches. A song-with-dialogue of 1809, 'The Mail Coach', gives the flavour.

> . . . I mount, the whip I crack now,
> All bustle, what a pack now
> On every side approach;
> Now making sad grimaces
> All for the want of places,
> They cry, I've lost the coach.

How's this? I'm sure my name was booked. – I don't see it, ma'am.
No room for two ladies. None at all for females; this is a mail
coach . . . Hip!

Cruikshank shows a coach about to overset – and silence a newsman

among others. Cruikshank's friend William Clarke describes the scene:

'A knot of cads, coachmen, old women, butchers'-boys and all those droll but true creatures who are usual in his sketches are scrambling, tossing, tumbling and fighting in most terrific confusion . . . In the centre of the group appears a Life-Guardsman, with his head, shoulders and half his body boldly visible above the heads of the belligerents. He is walking through them with calm dignity, his head erect and his eye just glancing down his cheek at the row below . . . He pursues his steady course through the squabble like a seventy-four sailing among a crew of cock-boats. I told George that the fellow was fine; but it took me half an hour to bring him to my way of thinking. His objection was, that one of the Life-Guards may be seen so acting in a similar situation every day of the week.'[108]

AN INTERESTING SCENE ON BOARD AN EAST-INDIAMAN, SHOWING THE EFFECTS
OF A HEAVY LURCH, AFTER DINNER
9 November 1818

A great many unpleasant things are happening. The man at the lefthand end of the table has his head bashed against a gun. The woman next to him is losing her wig. Two places further on, a man is getting scalding coffee down his throat and a boot in the stomach, and a dog is biting his calf. A negro servant is the victim of a bowl of hot punch. Only three old seadogs are at ease: the captain in the background, the sailor by the gun ('My precious eyes Tom!!! here's a smash!!!! hold on my hearties!! hang on by your eyelids.') and his mate swigging from a bottle.

Etched from a drawing by Captain Frederick Marryat, the author of *Mr Midshipman Easy*.

ROYAL HOBBIES, OR THE HERTFORDSHIRE COCK-HORSE!
20 April 1819

As soon as the newly-invented velocipede, also known as the hobby, became the craze of London early in 1819, it was used in political caricatures (just as the balloon was in 1785). This magnificently double-loaded machine is one of the finest images of the Regent and his mistress Lady Hertford. Her medallion is of St George and the dragon, a further hint of her commanding role (see commentary on 'The Belle Alliance'). The Regent's grumbling was not wide of the mark: his eye was roving and he was about to abandon her.

The double meanings in the dialogue are made explicit in a very similar print by a rival caricaturist, J. L. Marks, in which Lady Hertford says: 'You idle fellow, I'll make you *drive it home*! You shall remember *pushing* your *hobby* in Hertford!!!'

The Duke of York, off to Windsor in the background (see next page), has a word of caution for his brother and the marchioness, 'I had a tumble,' meaning his Mary Anne Clarke scandal.

The Duke of York has two hobbies besides his velocipede: his mistress, Mrs Carey, who lived at Fulham; and a 'devilish snug' sinecure job arranged for him after Queen Charlotte's death in 1818. This was to pay a monthly visit to his mad, blind father at Windsor Castle for the enormous sum of £10,000 a year (his fat saddlebag) in addition to his regular income, which is probably understated on the paper sticking from his pocket saying '£60,000 pr annm'. He was so enormously in debt, mainly through obsessive gambling, that the £10,000 merely helped to pay his interest.

When the duke says he wishes his army had had hobbies in Flanders, he means on the two disastrous expeditions he led in the 1790s. Mrs Carey plays on the phrase 'coming York', meaning cheating or overreaching. The widespread anger over the £10,000 is expressed by a grim countryman with starving children, who quotes Hamlet's 'unweeded garden' speech.

DANDIES DRESSING
2 November 1818

One of a number of caricatures done jointly by George and his brother Robert when they shared the studio in the old family home in Dorset Street. By 1818 the dandies have become more ridiculous than ever, especially round the neck. As Thomas Moore says of them:

> Quite a new sort of creatures, unknown yet to
>   scholars,
> With heads so immovably stuck in shirt-collars
> That seats like our music-stools soon must be
>   found them
> To twirl, when the creatures may wish to look
>   round them! [109]

Another problem is pointed out by the dandy on the left: 'D--n it, I really believe I must take off my cravat or I shall never get my trousers on.' (His left foot was surely drawn by George.)

There is a good satirical picture of the start of a dandy's day in a book of 1819:

> Waked at three p.m. at Long's [a fashionable May-fair hotel] . . . Ordered some chocolate, but could not get it down: drank three glasses of Danzig brandy. Thought I looked d----d well, after shaving, washing my face in olympian dew, putting on a little of the *light brown* and a touch of *rouge* to give a lustre to my eye . . . Musked myself highly and put white wax in my nails. Sent to Pall Mall for Scott's [the tailor's] foreman and kept him an hour instructing him how to pad my coat on the breast and on the shoulders, to put very thick lining and padding in the sleeves . . . and to come down taper at the wrist like a lady's sleeve . . . Put on my stays; broke three laces . . . [110]

But the padded bottoms and bosomy tops were not to last much longer. The assertion of a supreme purposelessness had a last fling, at a time of much writing about utility and campaigning about reform, before giving way to the more convenient modes of the nineteenth-century majority.

A turning of the tide can be detected in the work of Henry Luttrell, a high-society versifier. At first his hero Charles is:

> Just like an hour-glass or a wasp,
> So tightened he could scarcely gasp.
> Cold was the nymph who did not dote
> Upon him in his new-built coat;
> Whose heart could parry the attacks
> Of those voluminous cossacks. [*trousers*]

He is as anxious as any dandy to get the yards of muslin wound round his collar to perfection:

> 'Have you, my friend,' I've heard him say,
> 'Been lucky with your turns today?'

But then he is smitten by Julia, a sensible girl who despises the dandies' excesses. He is a changed man:

> No more he bears a bosom full
> Of buckram, or o'ercharged with wool . . .
> He looks, poor fellow, less genteelly,
> 'Tis certain, but he moves more freely. [111]

When Captain Rees Gronow years later set down his reminiscences of those days, when he himself had moved in the best society, this was his verdict: 'How unspeakably odious – with a few brilliant exceptions, such as Alvanley and others – were the dandies of forty years ago! They were a motley crew . . . generally not high-born, nor rich, nor very good-looking, nor clever, nor agreeable . . . had large appetites and weak digestions, gambled freely and had no luck. They hated everybody and abused everybody . . . swore a good deal, never laughed, had their own particular slang, looked hazy after dinner . . .' [112]

LANDING THE TREASURES, OR RESULTS OF THE POLAR EXPEDITION!!!
18 January 1819

Captain Marryat and Cruikshank collaborated here in mocking a seagoing venture, Commander John Ross's expedition to Baffin Bay in 1818. The plump commander marches pompously at the head of a procession of seamen disconsolately carrying arctic trophies to the British Museum (in its former building, Montagu House). All of them have lost their noses and ears by frostbite; Ross wears an artificial nose. He is greeted by a violin-playing busker, the negro Billy Waters, a noted London character, singing, 'O captain he is come to town, doodle doodle dandy . . .' Among the specimens are a bear, red snow (Ross brought some home, melted, in a bottle), 'worms found in the intestines of a seal', and an alleged Eskimo, who carries an artist's portfolio. A bulldog lifts its leg to some worried-looking Eskimo dogs. One of the people cheering on the museum wall is the naturalist Sir Joseph Banks, who shouts, 'Huzza! they have got Ursus Major, as I live.'

A VISIT TO COCKNEY FARM—VIEWING THE GROUNDS

25 May 1819

Another non-political laugh from an idea by Captain Marryat. The pretensions of new-rich townees were a frequent source of humour. The ribaldry about all the dung and water that the Cockney has been making is pointed up by the outdoor privy at right. The dandy is losing his boots and can hardly take in the double-meaning suggestion of the wife. The child is in grave danger from a duck.

[73]

THE HOBBY HORSE DEALER
25 July 1819

The threat from new technology dismays the ostler and the horses. The dandies – who were associated with the velocipede as soon as it came in – discuss the machine as if it were a horse. A notice on the stable says, 'A fine stud of *real horses* to be sold as cheap as dog's meat.' In the background a lady and gentleman propel themselves past in a cloud of dust, followed by a sullen groom.

An earlier velocipede had been tried in Paris about 1813. A London man launched an improved version in 1818, and this caricature of July 1819 – devised by another friend of Cruikshank's, John Sheringham – comes at about the height of the vogue. The London magistrates condemned the thing as a danger to pedestrians; and anyway it was too much like hard work, especially for dandies. Horses survived.

DAMN ALL THINGS

1819-21

THE BELLE ALLIANCE, OR THE FEMALE REFORMERS OF BLACKBURN!!!　　12 August 1819

It was bad enough, rightminded people thought, when working-men began to hold mass political meetings, as they did in the summer of 1819, especially in the Midlands and Lancashire. But when organized Female Union Societies emerged, a collapse of the old order seemed near. (It was not improper, of course, for women to do a long day's work in the mines.) Cruikshank's caricature for the conservative George Humphrey is based on a report in a radical paper, *The Black Dwarf*, of a meeting at which a cap of liberty (the French revolutionary symbol) was presented by the women reformers of Blackburn, Lancashire. Cruikshank deals with the unsettling thought of aggressive

women by making nearly all of them hideous and putting them in breeches. And he turns the whole threat into a sexual laugh. The placing of the cap of liberty on the pole of the reform banner becomes a lewd action: the woman asks 'every man in England to *stand up* & come forward & *join* the *general union*, that by a *determined constitutional resistance* to our *oppressors* we may obtain the *great end!!!*'

The petticoat banner, labelled 'The Female St George overcoming the Monster Corruption', is just as lewd. The dragon is on his back and the woman straddles him: an allusion to an old slang phrase, 'riding St George', for the woman's taking the superior position.

[77]

ROYAL EMBARKATION

OR BEARING BRITANNIA'S HOPE FROM A BATHING MACHINE TO THE ROYAL BARGE

19 August 1819

A week later, at Thomas Tegg's printshop at the other end of town, Cruikshank mocks the Regent, the symbol of state stability. His *two* royal yachts, both fitted with the greatest luxury, were another example of his impolitic squandering. Here he is seen about to be conveyed to one of them at Brighton for a trip to the Cowes regatta. As a Fairburn pamphlet, *The R---l Cruise, or Half Seas Over ! !*, said on an earlier occasion –

> Crowds gazing stand upon the beach
> The while the royal troop from Steine
> Embark by means of bath machine.

The little wheeled houses known as bathing machines, from which the well-to-do used to plunge into the sea, were useful for embarkations as well – and for other things, Cruikshank suggests with his pair of plump girls, 'The best *machines* in Brighton'. Although the Regent is in a nervous state, his left hand follows its royal instincts. The other bathing-woman makes a political point: 'Faith, he's no joke, Judy, the devil a heavier *burthen in all the country* ! !'

[78]

MASSACRE AT ST PETER'S, OR 'BRITONS STRIKE HOME'!!!
August 1819

The political agitation in the north had its climax in the event that was quickly christened the Peterloo Massacre: on 16 August 1819 a force of yeomanry cavalry backed by regular troops broke up a meeting of fifty thousand people at Manchester, killing eleven and wounding hundreds. Cruikshank pictures the yeomanry as butchers in uniform, with meat cleavers in their hands and steels at their belts – which was not far from the truth, for most of them were small shopkeepers or farmers, men terrified by the new militancy of the poor.

A RADICAL REFORMER, i.e. A NECK OR NOTHING MAN! Dedicated to the HEADS of the nation
17 September 1819

Peterloo deepened the public distaste for the Regent and for his mediocre ministers, and all the more so when the Home Secretary, Lord Sidmouth, conveyed to the Manchester magistrates the 'great satisfaction' of the Regent at their 'prompt, decisive and efficient measures'. But how could decent middle-class people ally themselves with radical reformers? Only thirty years after the fall of the Bastille, many feared it might be Britain's turn. Cruikshank reflects the anger and the fear. His terrifying 'neck or nothing man' was not only issued by the same printseller as the St Peter's Massacre; the surviving sketches show that it was designed on the same piece of paper.

Where does Cruikshank stand? Not with the radicals; but not with the government either. It is hard to know whether to take the guillotine-monster seriously. Perhaps Cruikshank, like Gillray in some of his prints, was happy to let different buyers take things in different ways. But nobody is asked to have any sympathy for the Regent, leading the stampede despite his gouty foot; or Lord Liverpool, falling to the ground over his and Castlereagh's bags of gold; or Castlereagh, saying, 'I don't like the looks of him at all, at all!'; or Lord Chancellor Eldon, telling the Regent not to mind losing his wig 'so long as your *head's* on!'

LOYAL ADDRESSES & RADICAL PETITIONS,
OR THE R----T'S MOST GRACIOUS ANSWER TO BOTH SIDES OF THE QUESTION AT ONCE
4 December 1819

In the months following Peterloo, the government and its followers organized loyal addresses to the Regent to counteract a mass of petitions for a Peterloo inquiry (there never was one) and for political reform. Here the Regent thanks a smooth-looking set of gentlemen declaring their support of 'your Royal Highness & the present order of things'. 'Kiss my hand,' he says – and gives his answer another way to the petitioners. The man holding his nose is Sir Francis Burdett, reformist MP for Westminster. To supplement the joke, there is a Regent's Bomb in full blast, and an open book, 'The Art of Killing Two Birds with One Stone, by F. Fartardo'.

The same bitter joke about petitioners being royally answered 'the backward way' had been used fifty years before in a caricature set in the Regent's father's throne-room. Men born in John Wilkes's time must have wondered if anything would ever change.

Within the illustration:

Mr Bull removed by the Tax Gatherers over the Way.

Freedom of the Press — Transportation

PRAY Remember the poor DEBTORS

NO GRUMBLING

Tampering at Elections — allowed to Ministers only!! Lord Lieutenants of Counties & other Local Authorities must be tools of Government for Necessary Purposes, employ Clerical Magistrates

Free discussion — a farce

Right of Petitioning, reserved to Families only

MAGNA CHARTA

LAW of LIBEL

Bill of RIGHTS

A FREE BORN ENGLISHMAN!
THE ADMIRATION OF THE WORLD!!!
AND THE ENVY OF SURROUNDING NATIONS!!!!!
15 December 1819

Peterloo and the furore that followed were used by the government to justify the passage of new measures, the Six Acts, which went even further than in 1817 to gag free speech. Political organizing and public meetings were virtually banned; the newspaper tax, whose purpose was to make papers too dear for common people, was extended to a wide range of cheap newssheets, and it was made illegal to sell them for less than sixpence; and severe new penalties were imposed for alleged seditious publishing. Padlocked, ragged John Bull wears shackles from waist to ankles like those that were now being clamped on men arrested for selling dissident pamphlets. In his bound hands he clutches, with his pen, a paper saying 'Freedom of the press — transportation': for a second offence of seditious publication, a man could now be transported to Botany Bay.

> Now *right* consists in breaking bones;
>   In *yeoman's* swords to cut and slay —

says a pamphlet published by Fairburn.[113]

> To keep him ignorant of his rights
>   The *twopenny trash* is doom'd to die —

meaning William Cobbett's *Political Register* and other radical weekly papers selling for twopence.

> John Bull through twenty years of war
>   To liberty had some pretences —

this was the most telling complaint of all: no array of repressive laws had been needed like these now created in peacetime to deal with what was called 'treason and impiety'.

In the background is a scene of poverty and starvation. The man walking past the imprisoned debtors is demonstrating that he cannot help them: he himself has not even pockets to his coat.

This print had a great vogue. Eighteen months later the attorney-general was denouncing it in the Commons as 'an indecent caricature'.

DEATH OR LIBERTY! OR BRITANNIA & THE VIRTUES OF THE CONSTITUTION IN DANGER
OF VIOLATION FROM THE GREAT POLITICAL LIBERTINE, RADICAL REFORM!

1 December 1819

The title sounds self-mocking; yet when Cruikshank engraved this blow at the radicals for Humphrey, he added to his usual signature the formula *invt. et fect.*, indicating that he personally devised it. Was he specially pleased, then, with his image of Radical Reform, a masked death-figure with grotesque genitals, attempting to rape a valiant Britannia? Beneath the radical cloak march a fearsome tribe: Murder, Robbery, Starvation, Slavery, Blasphemy (with Paine's *Age of Reason*, a book whose vendors were being jailed) and Immorality. Might Cruikshank have been willing for these creatures to be taken, by those who so wished, as a mockery of extreme anti-radical propaganda?

[83]

The three wood engravings on these pages are from *The Political House That Jack Built*, the first enormously popular Hone/Cruikshank pamphlet, issued in December 1819 (see page 15). The Regent is not much caricatured, yet he is the picture of pompous folly. The substitution of delicate peacock feathers for the usual Prince of Wales feathers perfects the message. The corkscrew dangling among the other orders is a touch first used by Gillray twenty-seven years earlier in his famous engraving of the already bloated prince, 'A Voluptuary under the Horrors of Digestion'. Hone's accompanying verses read:

> This is THE MAN – all shaven and shorn,
> All cover'd with Orders – and all forlorn;
> THE DANDY OF SIXTY,
>   who bows with a grace,
> And has *taste* in wigs, collars,
>   cuirasses and lace;

THE DANDY OF SIXTY

> Who to tricksters and fools
>   leaves the State and its treasure,
> And when Britain's in tears
>   sails about at his pleasure . . .

In writing these lines, Hone may well have had in mind a passage in a book he had just published, William Hazlitt's *Political Essays*. Hazlitt says a prince may be 'a man of good nature and good manners, graceful in his person, the idol of the other sex; . . . he may be an excellent mimic; he may say good things, and do friendly ones; he may be able to join in a catch, or utter a repartee, or dictate a billet-doux; . . . he may have an equal taste in ragouts and poetry, in dancing, and in dress; he may adjust a toupee with the dexterity of a friseur, or tie a cravat with the hand and eye of a man-milliner; he may have all these graces and accomplishments . . . and yet he may be nothing.'[114] Those who come next have fewer graces:

> These are THE PEOPLE all tatter'd and torn,
> Who curse the day
>   wherein they were born . . .
> Who peaceably meeting
>   to ask for Reform,
> Were sabred by Yeomanry Cavalry, who
> Were thank'd by THE MAN,
>   all shaven and shorn . . .

In the foreground is an evicted family: a stool and jug lie beside them. In the background, Peterloo. Together, a fitting image for Shelley's line, 'A people starved and stabbed in the untilled field', in his sonnet of 1819 that begins, 'An old, mad, blind, despised and dying king'.

THE PEOPLE

[Full page from *The Political House
That Jack Built*]

Church of England clergymen, or at least the well-
endowed senior clergy, had long been little venerated;
and during the Regency many a vicar earned the
hatred of humbler people for the way he performed
his second role of magistrate. Here Hone introduces
such a man, who –

> Beggars and paupers
>   incessantly teases;
> Commits starving vagrants,
>   and orders distress
> On the poor for their rates;
>   signs warrants to press,
> And beats up for names
>   to a Loyal Address;
> Would indict for rebellion
>   those who petition;
> And all who look peaceable
>   try for sedition . . .
> And order the soldiers
>   'to aid and assist',
> That is – kill the helpless
>   who cannot resist . . .
> On God turns his back
>   when he turns the State's agent;
> And damns his own soul
>   to be friends with the [Regent].

Hone's shilling pamphlet quickly brought forth
counter-pamphlets. One depicts a quite different
priest, 'the friend of the poor', denouncing 'blas-
phemers and hollow deceivers' and

> Exhorting the poor to hold fast by the Bible,
> And leave all the rest to the children of libel;
> To look up to Him to whom mercy belongs
> To protect them from ill and redress all their wrongs.

The Regent, too, is another man altogether

> Who views with disdain, or a good-humour'd smile,
> The libellous trash of the base and the vile.[115]

In fact he was repeatedly exhorting his law officers to
prosecute; and bribing those satirists who could be
bribed.

THE CLERICAL MAGISTRATE.

" *The Bishop.* Will you be diligent in Prayers—laying aside the study of the
world and the flesh ?——*The Priest.* I will.
The Bishop. Will you maintain and set forwards, as much as lieth in you,
quietness, peace, and love, among all Christian People ?——*Priest.* I will.
¶ The Bishop laying his hand upon the head of him that receiveth the order
of Priesthood, shall say, RECEIVE THE HOLY GHOST."
The Form of Ordination for a Priest.

———— " The pulpit (in the sober use
Of its legitimate peculiar pow'rs)
Must stand acknowledg'd, while the world shall stand,
The most important and effectual guard,
Support, and ornament of virtue's cause.

Behold the picture! Is it like ?

THIS IS A PRIEST,

made ' according to Law'.

Go H—df—t, Y—rm—th, C—le—gh, and C—nn—g,

Go, and be planning,

Within your virtuous minds, what best will answer

To save *our* morals from this public cancer;

Go and impress, my friends, upon all classes,

From sleek-fac'd Swindlers down to half-starv'd Asses,

" That, from religious principles alone,"

(*Don't be such d—d fools as to blab your own*),

Temperance, chasteness, conjugal attention—

With other virtues that I need not mention—

And from subordination, and respect,

To every knave in robes of office deck'd—

" Can they expect to gain divine protection"

And save their sinful bodies from dissection !

[from THE MAN IN THE MOON, December 1819]

This is a page from Hone and Cruikshank's next pamphlet, *The Man in the Moon*, published before Christmas 1819. The scene is Lunataria, a place rather like Britain. Consider the Prince of Lunataria's procession to address his senators, 'that reverend body of Moonarian sages':

> Gods! what a sight! what countless crowds were there,
> What yells, and groans, and hootings, rent the air!
> By which, I learn'd, the Lunatarian nation
> Are wont to testify their admiration.

In a parody of the Speech from the Throne that led on to the passing of the Six Acts, the prince warns of conspirators:

> Reform, reform, the swinish rabble cry –
> Meaning, of course, rebellion, blood and riot –
> Audacious rascals! You, my lords, and I,
> Know 'tis their duty to be starved in quiet.

In the page reproduced here, the prince tells Lords Headfort and Yarmouth (two far from virtuous members of his court) and Castlereagh and Canning to urge religion upon the people. The phrases in quotation marks are from his actual speech; but the virtues he names are hardly his own. He is pictured on poor Lord Sidmouth's back, propped by Castlereagh, as he fires an ineffectual bursting blunderbuss at a winged liberty cap.

The prince tells his senators 'to check the circulation of little books':

> Oh! they are full of blasphemies and libels,
> And people read them oftener than their Bibles.

Cruikshank's illustration for this passage has Castlereagh, Canning and Sidmouth, armed with axe, noose, dagger and chains, trying to overcome a female liberty figure who defends a press. In his frontispiece Cruikshank shows the Regent holding up a tattered piece of cloth on the tip of his sword, in an effort – ineffectual, again – to black out the light of the world, a printing press blazing like the sun.

Hone's pamphlets brought other publishers to Cruikshank with similar ideas. Within a few weeks he had done twenty-three illustrations for *The Political 'A, Apple-Pie'* for James Johnston of Cheapside, a radical publisher for whom he had caricatured since 1811. This Johnston was not a scrupulous character. In April 1819 he had taken £95 of the royal money (see page 16) for suppressing three prints and promising not to publish 'any plate or matter' about the Regent. But in the *Political Apple-Pie*, which lists all the holders of lucrative public offices and gives verses on them, the letter P is illustrated by the Prince Regent who –

> Most graciously cast his own fine royal eye
> At the fruit and the crust of this great Apple-Pie!
> ... Oh, yes, though a leer, it was full of desire:
> Though merely a peep it was pregnant with fire.

Also under P are The People, who, when they asked for a bite,

> Got a kick o' their bottoms, which serv'd them just right;
> For 'twas properly ask'd, 'What have Peasants to do
> With a Pie, but to work hard, that others may chew?'

The verses gave Cruikshank a good idea for the letter B, illustrated here:

> The Bishops, God bless them, and bless all their wigs!
> They bit at this Pie like as many fat pigs.
> Though the bites that they made were none of them small,
> Great Barrington's greatly exceeded them all.

This meant the Hon Shute Barrington, Bishop of Durham – blessed with £19,000 a year. But an even juicier slice of the tax pie went to another man among the B's. Earl Bathurst, War Secretary and possessor of various sinecures, got £32,700, enough to pay the annual wages of more than 1,400 farm labourers. For him, and for many peers receiving lesser amounts for doing little or nothing, the public purse helped to consolidate the estates which many of their descendants still enjoy.

In 1820 the placemen and sinecurists – the Splendid Paupers, as they were called – were a hot issue for the reformers. Their names and takings were published by John Fairburn under the title *The Black Book, or Corruption Unmasked*. 'The aristocracy may be considered only one family, plundering, deluding and fattening on the people,' it says; 'and by its connexions possessing more power and influence in society than the ancient barons.' (It reckons that 144 peers nominate 300 of the 658 MPs; and a pamphlet of 1821, *Links of the Lower House*, says 402 MPs are related by blood or marriage to peers.)

Then there is the royal family. *The Black Book* reckons 'the mere personal cost of fourteen individuals' at £1,078,997 a year, and asks, 'Ought the people quietly to submit to such abominable profusion, when agriculture and commerce are paralysed by taxation, and the industrious artisan is famishing on five shillings a week? ... What use are

they? What services do they render to the state? Do they fight its battles? Do they conduct its negotiations? Do they administer justice to the people?' The book demonstrates that America's spending on state officers, envoys and so forth is less than a twentieth of Britain's, and asks, 'Are men to be termed seditious because they complain of this heart-rending contrast? Are they to be termed incendiaries, anarchists and revolutionaries because they exclaim to a patient and suffering people – "There! there is the cause of your privations!"'

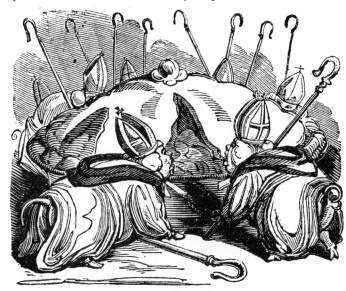

B–BIT IT
January 1820

"The Devil's in the Moon for mischief,
And yet she looks so modest all the while."

DON JUAN.

The LORD of the FAITHLESS.

———

" Me, miserable, which way shall I fly—
Infinite wrath, and infinite despair?
Which way I fly is Hell, myself am Hell;
And in the lowest depth, a lower deep
Still threat'ning to devour me, opens wide,
To which the Hell I suffer seems a Heaven.

[from THE MEN IN THE MOON, early 1820]

Cruikshank's contribution to the radical pamphlets was so much admired that people devising counter-pamphlets in defence of 'social order' turned to him – and he did not refuse. One riposte to Hone that he illustrated early in 1820 was *The Men in the Moon*, an attack on various questioners of things-as-they-were. Among these dangerous men is Lord Byron, whom the Poet Laureate, Robert Southey, and others were denouncing as a leader of the Satanic School of writing. Cruikshank depicts The Lord of the Faithless with a cloven hoof instead of his clubfoot. A winged devil is his guiding spirit – pointing him towards a gallows.

Closer to home, Cruikshank saucily shows his friend William Hone (right), lashed to a whipping-post with his partner the devil, being flogged by Castlereagh while Sidmouth and Canning watch approvingly. The ministers are of course nicer gentlemen than in Hone's pamphlets. Some accompanying verses refer to Hone's trials in 1817 for blasphemous libel (see page 15) and to a public subscription made for him (to which, incidentally, the Duke of Bedford and two Whig earls contributed a hundred guineas each):

Behold! the *Blasphemer*, of infamous fame . . .

A Printer and his Devil restrained.

Lucio "Why, how now, Claudio? when comes this restraint?
Claud. From too much liberty, my Lucio,—liberty.
  As surfeit is the father of much fast,
  So every scope, by the immoderate use,
  Turns to restraint."

BEHOLD! the *Blasphemer*, of infamous fame, ⎫
Who profaned sacred truth, to secure a base name, ⎬
And the bread of his blasphemy eats without shame; ⎭

D

[from THE MEN IN THE MOON]

THUS PERISH ALL
April 1820

It was appropriate in this picture of ministerial self-slaughter (from a radical pamphlet, *The Queen in the Moon*) to show Canning using pistols, for he had once fought a duel with Castlereagh; and to show Sidmouth hanging himself, for as Home Secretary he was much concerned with executions; but it was a remarkable prophetic stroke to show Castlereagh cutting his throat, for he did just that two years later, on 12 August 1822 (George IV's sixtieth birthday). The only reason he used not a razor but a penknife was that his razors had been taken away from him.

When Castlereagh (by then Lord Londonderry) killed himself, John Fairburn hurriedly printed a pamphlet on him and hunted for Cruikshank to illustrate it. A pencilled note survives that gives a glimpse of the way he was called upon for instant journalism:

Dear George – Fairburn has been here and wishes you to etch a small plate of Londonderry in the act of destroying himself for the frontispiece to a pamphlet but it must be done tomorrow and should your thumb prevent you he must he says go to your brother. The paragraph in the paper which he has left marked will furnish you with the necessary instructions.[116]

This was a paragraph telling how Londonderry fell dying into the arms of his doctor. Cruikshank did the plate.

QUALIFICATION
August 1820

George III's death in January 1820 turned the Regent into George IV –
and his wife into Queen Caroline. Instead of accepting £50,000 a year to
stay on the continent – where for five years she had been living, as she
put it, as 'a happy, merry soul' with her Italian lover – she returned to
England in June 1820 to insist on being accepted as queen to the man
who had refused to be seen near her for a quarter of a century. She
came with the encouragement of some leading reformers: she made
such a portentous problem for the newly-proclaimed and unloved
George IV. Instantly this battered, brandy-loving, unstable woman
became a heroine, 'the injured queen'. If she had erred, was it not her
sinful husband's fault? Even men who questioned the need for kings
became hot in her cause, though she was royal enough, being a niece of
George III. This saddened the anti-royalist William Hazlitt: 'Here were
all the patriots and Jacobins of London and Westminster, who scorned
and hated the king, going to pay their homage to the queen, and ready to
worship the very rags of royalty. The wives and daughters of popular
caricaturists and of forgotten demagogues were ready to pull caps in the
presence-chamber for precedence ... The world must have something to
admire, and the more worthless and stupid their idol is, the better.'[117]

It was a fine time for satirists. Hone's first idea for Cruikshank to
illustrate was *The Queen's Matrimonial Ladder*, a parody this time of a
pictorial piece of drollery about marriage. It takes George, as prince and
king, up and down fourteen steps, beginning with his 'Qualification'
for marriage in 1795:

> In love, and in drink, and o'ertoppled by debt;
> With women, with wine, and with duns on the fret.

This was the truth: in 1795 he was o'ertoppled by debts of well over
£600,000. Some years before, the nation had had to pay off a similarly
vast debt for him, and he had promised to behave; so he was rescued
only on condition that he married (aged thirty-three) and began to lead a
respectable life.

Cruikshank's drawing owes something to Gillray's 'Voluptuary
Under the Horrors of Digestion' of 1792. William Clarke much admired
it: 'This is "the most finished gentleman in Europe". Look at the floor ...
The star [of the Order of the Garter] has fallen; but the loose garter is
ready with the excuse – *Honi soit*, etc. How *very* drunk his Majesty is to
be sure! There's a bonnet on the corner of the screen, and three or four
bottles, or so, under the chair.'[118] Seven bottles, in fact; and cards,
dice and a satyr's mask. The screen displays three plump dancers, an
amorous Bacchus on an ass, and a flying goat of Wales. Beneath the
picture, Hone quoted Solomon: 'Give not thy strength unto women,
nor thy ways to that which destroyeth kings.'

George IV ordered his ministers to bring witnesses from Italy, prove
Caroline's adultery at a House of Lords hearing, and have her declared
unfit to be his queen. But what about his own list of adulteries, in which
a new marchioness, Conyngham, had just succeeded the old one of
Hertford? This pamphlet touches on the point:

Yet he thought to himself – 'twas a thought most distressing –
'If *she* should discover I've been M--ch----ss--g . . !'

Poor George is not kindly described:

> Fat, fifty-eight and frisky, still a beau . . .
> Led by a passion, prurient, blind and batter'd,
> Lame, bloated, pointless, flameless, aged and shatter'd;
> Creeping, like Guy Fawkes, to blow up his wife.

The last step of the ladder is 'Degradation': illustrated by the king in a white sheet, standing in church as a contrite sinner; and the three legible commandments are 'Thou shalt not commit adultery . . . Thou shalt not bear false witness . . . Thou shalt not covet thy neighbour's wife . . .' By this date Cruikshank had made his £100 undertaking not to depict George IV 'in any immoral situation'. What could be more moral than a repentant sinner?

And was it immoral to show him, 'lame, bloated, shattered', being wheeled along by a sturdy cupid crying 'Cat's meat!'?

'CAT'S MEAT'

Both these last scenes were deplored by the counter-attacking *Loyalist's Magazine*:

> What more degradation will Rhymer attempt?
> What farther abuse, from *treason* exempt?
> He sets him, hung round with a sheet, on a stool,
> For the finger of scorn to deride as a fool!
> . . . Till, fell'd and destroy'd by the radical crew,
> He is drawn in a barrow, the cats crying 'mew' ! !
> Shame, Britons! Awake! Shall your Monarch be hurl'd
> By radical scribblers, as *scum*, through the world![119]

He was indeed being exposed to the laughter of foreigners. The French published a pirated copy, *George Dandin ou l'Echelle Matrimoniale de la Reine d'Angleterre*; just as they had earlier published *La Maison Politique que Jacques a Batie*.

DEGRADATION

THE FAT IN THE FIRE
August 1820

Devils stoke the fire, and the king's famous haunches seem to be melting. This was one design remembered by William Maginn in his article on Cruikshank thirteen years later in *Fraser's Magazine*: 'Tories as we were and are, and as we trust we still shall be, these comic picturings [of George IV and his friends] haunt our imagination. The poor old king in every attitude of ludicrous distress (the ''Fat in the Fire'' was perfection); ... Castlereagh (but even the professed caricaturist could not destroy the gentlemanly grace of that noble face and figure); the ''Waterloo man'' with his sword dropping into the scale against the pen; the various parsons, jailors, jockeys, lawyers and the rest, were first-rate.' [120]

The Fat in the Fire illustrates a Hone lampoon of September 1820, *Non Mi Ricordo*, an adroit parody of some of the earlier sessions of the Caroline 'trial' in the Lords, which was reported at length day after day (quadrupling the circulation of the steam-printed *Times*, on good days, to an astonishing 32,000). The crafty Henry Brougham, cross-examining for the queen, led one of the Italian witnesses into saying repeatedly, '*Non mi ricordo*' (I don't remember). It became a catch-phrase. Hone puts the king himself under questioning:

How much money has been expended on you since you were born?
    Non mi ricordo...
Are you married? More yes than no...
Why did you marry? To pay my debts.
Then why did you part? Because my debts were paid...
After that what did you do? Oh, I rambled about.
Where did you go? To [Lady] Jersey and elsewhere.
Well, sir, go on. Non mi ricordo.
Do you mean to say that you never went to Manchester Square?
    More yes than no...
Is the Marquis of C. a married man?
                    (Order. Order.)
... Are you a sober man? More no than yes.
How many bottles a day do you drink? Non mi ricordo...
How many nights in the week do you go to bed sober?
    Non mi ricordo.
Are you sober now? More no than yes.

Hone's pamphlets were read not only by the lower and middle classes. Wellington's intimate friend, Mrs Charles Arbuthnot, whose Toryism more than matched his, says that Lord Duncannon, a fellow-guest at the Earl of Westmorland's, had a copy of *Non Mi Ricordo*. She calls it 'very ridiculous and clever ... not so ill-humoured as most of those things usually are now'.[121] She deplored George IV, knowing how poor Wellington suffered from his tantrums and double-dealing.

DOLL TEAR-SHEET,

ALIAS THE

Countess 'Je ne me rappelle pas,'

A MATCH FOR

"NON MI RICORDO."

With Cuts.

I shall make it spin as long as I can

KEEPING IT UP!!

[title-page, DOLL TEAR-SHEET, September 1820]

MARQUIS OF CUCKOLDOM,
ALIAS THE CORNUTED ANIMAL!!!
September 1820

A French ex-servant of Caroline also had an uncertain memory, and Hone's rival, John Fairburn, put out a pamphlet on her. This was Cruikshank's title-page design. The king, in fool's cap, tries to keep the Constitution top spinning. His bottle is labelled Imbecility. 'Keeping it up' means prolonging a debauch.

Cruikshank's final illustration to *Doll Tear-Sheet*, 'Marquis of Cuckoldom', is a clear violation of his £100 pledge. The king is seen on a seat outside his Nash-built cottage at Windsor, where he secluded himself during most of the Caroline uproar. (Mrs Arbuthnot says the Guards 'were all drinking the queen's health & had the greatest possible contempt for the king, thinking him a coward & afraid of showing himself'.)[122] The woman perched on his knee can only be the wife of the man in the foreground; and he of course is the Marquis Conyngham, who with good reason is saying 'God save great George our King'. He did not achieve a dukedom, but in return for smiling upon the king's passion for Lady Conyngham (the 'new old lady', a mere fifty-one), a British title was added to his Irish one. He became Lord Steward, his son Francis was made a Gentleman of the Bedchamber and later a Foreign Under-Secretary; and best of all, his wife was loaded with jewels (£100,000 in her first two years, it was estimated by the Privy Purse, Benjamin Bloomfield; and in fact the bills of only two jewellers for only part of her ten-year reign came to £127,849). At 58, George was as distracted over Lady Conyngham as he had been over Lady Hertford at the onset of that love a dozen years before. Mrs Arbuthnot records: 'They spend the evening sitting on a sofa together, holding each other's hands, whispering & kissing, Lord Conyngham being present.'[123] The Russian ambassador's wife, Princess Lieven, wrote cattily to Metternich: 'Not an idea in her head; nothing but a hand to accept pearls and diamonds with, and an enormous balcony to wear them on.'[124]

Perhaps Cruikshank was purging the crime of 'Marquis of Cuckoldom' when he did a full-page etching the following month for a pamphlet 'printed at the expense of the Loyal Association' (anti-radical things were selling so badly just then that they had to be subsidized). This was *The Radical Ladder, or Hone's Political Ladder and his Non Mi Ricordo Explained and Applied*. Its frontispiece shows Caroline, flaming torch in hand, mounting to the top rung (Mob Government) of a ladder and reaching out to grasp the crown, which is on top of a King/Lords/Commons pillar. Under cover of her vast cloak, a horde of wicked radicals follow, one of them waving a Democratic Republic banner.

The dreadful sequel is 'The Funeral Pile', illustrated here. Caroline, not George, wears the fool's cap. She has been enthroned by the radicals; they make a bonfire of all that Britons hold dear (Laws and Religion can be seen in the flames) and destroy the pillar and herself.

> And Rhymer is there, with his pamphlets to help,
> And the little Black Dwarf his applauses to yelp!
> 'Down with kings and with queens' is th'uproarious cry,
> 'Now we scorn our designs to disguise or deny.'[125]

These verses in the text of *The Radical Ladder* gave Cruikshank hints for his illustration. The Black Dwarf – Thomas Jonathan Wooler, editor of the radical paper of that name – is the one with the bellows. The Rhymer – William Hone – is the top figure on the ladder. But a strange touch is that the second cheering figure on the ladder is Cruikshank himself. One might read this as saying to Hone, Don't take this too seriously.

THE
RIGHT DIVINE OF KINGS TO GOVERN WRONG!

Dedicated to the Holy Alliance

BY THE AUTHOR OF
THE POLITICAL HOUSE THAT JACK BUILT.

" The devil will not have me damn'd, lest the *oil* that is in me should set hell on fire."
SHAKSPEARE.

LONDON:
PRINTED FOR WILLIAM HONE,
45, LUDGATE-HILL.
1821.

Eighteenpence.

The furore over Caroline, which for a time united radicals and Whigs, persuaded more and more peers that they would be wiser not to give George IV what he wanted, and in November 1820 the action against Caroline was dropped. By early 1821 she was no longer a heroine – especially when she accepted £50,000 a year after all. Hone returned to an earlier theme, his detestation of the Holy Alliance, and published an updated version of Daniel Defoe's *Jure Divino* of 1706, entitled *The Right Divine of Kings to Govern Wrong*! (a line from Pope's *Dunciad*).

Cruikshank's frontispiece was clearly inspired by a passage in Hone's preface: 'Kingcraft rears up its terrific mass, muffled in the mantle of Legitimacy; its head cowled and crowned, and dripping with the oil of Divine Rights; its eyes glaring deadly hate to human happiness; its lips demanding worship for itself.' Point was added by the fact that within a few months George IV was to be anointed at his coronation. The serrated sword and the bristly head are perhaps more comical than fearsome; but the sceptre topped by a skull with a fool's cap is a good touch, and so is the pair of nooses for genitals.

In this tailpiece to *The Right Divine*, the anointed tyrant has become an iron monster, his head a crowned cannonball with an aureole of daggers, his body a mortar, his arms and thighs shackles, his lower legs cannons. He tramples his victims and attacks a frail Tree of Liberty.

These are Cruikshank's metamorphoses of four of George IV's ministers for the next Cruikshank-Hone collaboration, *The Political Showman – at Home!* of April 1821. The Showman is an animated printing press and the pamphlet opens with his sideshow patter: 'Walk *up*! walk *up*! and see the curiosities and creatures – all alive! alive O!... Take care! Don't go within their reach – they mind nobody but *me*! A short time ago they got loose and... deperately attacked a Lady of Quality [Caroline]... *I'm in continual danger from 'em myself* – for if I didn't watch 'em closely they'd *destroy* ME... His Majesty is so *fond* of 'em that he often sees 'em *in private*, and *feeds* 'em...' The Showman claims the credit for the collapse of the Caroline trial; and the pamphlet has a full-page reproduction of a contribution by Cruikshank to London's celebration of that event: a large illuminated scene, painted on transparent material and displayed above Hone's shop at 45 Ludgate Hill, showing a goddess of liberty and a press, irradiated with the light of truth, casting Wellington, Liverpool, Sidmouth, Castlereagh and others into outer darkness.

A *PRIME* CRUTCH.—

(From the Westminster Infirmary—Upper Ward).

HE fondly ' IMITATES' that wondrous LAD,
   That durst assay the sun's bright flaming team;
Spite of whose feeble hands, the horses mad
   Fling down on burning earth the scorching beam;—
      So MADE *the flame in which* HIMSELF *was fired;*
      THE WORLD THE BONFIRE WAS—*when* HE *expired!**
   Like HIM of Ephesus, HE HAD WHAT HE DESIRED.
                              Fletcher's Purple Island.

* The 'LAD' died in the midst of war, ejaculating heaven to save the country from the miseries of his system of misrule.

A PRIME CRUTCH

A SCORPION

A SCORPION: This is Wellington. His presence in the Cabinet since 1818, with an army at his command more than three times the size of the peacetime army that Britain had had before the French Revolution, was seen by radicals as a threat of military government.

A PRIME CRUTCH: The uninspired prime minister, Lord Liverpool. The infirmary is parliament; the upper ward, the House of Lords. With each creature, Hone provided fitting quotations from his wide reading. Here we see part of what was applied to Liverpool. He is attacked for having pursued William Pitt's policy of destroying Napoleon at any cost. The passage about the Icarus-like 'wondrous Lad' is applied to Pitt: 'The world the bonfire was – when he expired!' By the time the war ended, Britain was burdened with a debt of about £1,000 million – one cause of the prolonged postwar distress.

Liverpool's exaggerated bag-wig represents his emoluments of £13,000, a fine sum then.

THE DOCTOR

DIRKPATRICK

THE DOCTOR: Sidmouth, Home Secretary, who had been nicknamed The Doctor twenty years before by the satirical George Canning; the reason for the name being that his father had been physician to the elder Pitt, and Sidmouth had made use of the connection to advance himself with the son. Cruikshank makes Sidmouth's body a doctor's enema bag (a thing that is always pictured with Sidmouth in Cruikshank's other caricatures of him).

DIRKPATRICK: Castlereagh, a more forceful man than Liverpool, was in effect prime minister, being in charge of the Commons (and its pecuniary management) as well as Foreign Secretary. Cruikshank shows him as a bloody dagger, wielding the lash that had long been his symbol, and holding a bleeding shamrock – both alluding to Castlereagh's allegedly bloody role as Chief Secretary in Ireland during the suppression of the rebels in 1798.

Castlereagh was noted for the suavity of his manners; and beneath the dagger-Castlereagh, Hone quoted Byron: 'I never judge from *manners*, for I once had my pocket picked by the *civilest* gentleman I ever met with.'

A few months after this was published, Castlereagh went to Dublin with George IV. The king was greeted with adulation, inspired partly by the idea that he might favour Catholic emancipation. Byron wrote (not for immediate publication):

Spread, spread for Vitellius the royal repast
Till the gluttonous despot be stuff'd to the gorge!

And the roar of his drunkards proclaim him at last
The Fourth of the fools and oppressors call'd George!
. . . Let the wine flow around the old bacchanal's throne,
Like their blood which has flow'd, and which yet has to flow.

As for Castlereagh, he is 'a wretch . . . reptile . . . miscreant':

See the cold-blooded serpent, with venom full flush'd,
Still warming its folds in the breast of a king![126]

Hazlitt too saw something reptilian in Castlereagh. He wrote in January 1821: 'He sits in the House of Commons, with his hat slouched over his forehead, and a sort of stoop in his shoulders . . . There is an irregular grandeur about him, an unwieldy power, loose, disjointed . . . coiled up in the folds of its own purposes – cold, deathlike, smooth and smiling – that is neither quite at ease with itself, nor safe for others to approach!'[127] Not at ease with itself: an astute perception.

In the pamphlet's frontispiece and its final illustration, Cruikshank reaches out to continental targets. The frontispiece is a nasty black bird of prey with six heads – the Holy Alliance, including the Pope. The other is a terrible dragon-like monster, the Legitimate Vampire, breathing blood and devouring the people. After describing the monster's cruel and rapacious habits, Hone says: 'His existence is drawing to a close. It has been ascertained that the way of putting him quietly out of the world is by a Black Dose . . . of the alphabet, properly composed,' which is to be 'forced down his throat *daily*, morning and evening, and on every seventh day a double dose should be administered'.

THE NEW TIMES

THE FINE OLD SUBSCRIPTION VESSEL,
THE REGENT'S BOMB

The last satirical work on which Hone and Cruikshank collaborated, before Hone turned away from politics, was *A Slap at Slop and the Bridge-Street Gang*, published August 1821. Like the illustrated pamphlets, this was an innovation: a mock-newspaper, illustrated with twenty-six wood engravings.

Slop is Hone's name for John Stoddart, Hazlitt's brother-in-law, a one-time revolutionary enthusiast who (as greater men had done) became a strong conservative. In 1818 Stoddart was dismissed as editor of *The Times* because the language in which he wrote about almost everything except royalty, Tories and the Holy Alliance was so abusive that it became ridiculous and was losing readers. With government aid he then launched *The New Times*, in which he carried on as before. Hone calls Stoddart's paper 'Royal Red Hot Slop . . . spooned out every morning . . . at 153 Fleet Street'. Cruikshank pictures Stoddart as an old woman selling a drink called saloop (sassafras tea), a common sight then. His brazier is an upturned crown, his container a slop-pail. The portly

gentleman enjoying the stuff is of course George IV, whom Cruikshank had taken to picturing as Great Boots. A lesser mortal who has swallowed some is leaving with a pain in his belly.

The second chief target is the Constitutional Association, formed the previous December to bring private prosecutions against radical papers and pamphlets which the Attorney-General thought it prudent to ignore because juries could no longer be counted upon to convict. Soon after *The Political House That Jack Built* was published, Hone was told, the Regent laid a copy on the table before the Privy Council; but when he had left, someone said, 'We have had enough of William Hone'. A year later, George IV sent some lampoons or caricatures on himself to Eldon and the Attorney-General and wrote: 'If the law as it now stands has not the power to protect the Sovereign against licentious abominations of this description, it is *high time* that the *law* should be *amended*.'[128] But the government had incurred enough odium for its new restraints on the press and free speech, and shied away from

'THE DAMNABLE ASSOCIATION';
OR THE INFERNAL INQUISITION OF BLACKFRIARS

THE TRIANGLE

prosecuting, let alone seeking wider powers against satire than had ever been needed before.

The Constitutional Association, nicknamed by Hone 'the Bridge-Street Gang' from its address near Blackfriars Bridge, was the alternative, warmly supported by George IV, which is why he is The Fine Old Subscription Vessel. He becomes the hull of a new royal yacht, with petticoats for sails, and the Regent's Bomb mounted in a fitting place.

The association was hard at work when *A Slap at Slop* was being created. Whig MPs attacked the association in the Commons; Samuel Whitbread said it was 'nothing less than an inquisition on the press'. Cruikshank took the hint. He shows a band of inquisitors at work in a dungeon, illuminated by a crown whose rays are labelled Places, Pensions, Preferments, Promotions, Rank . . . all the things that stimulated noble and gentlemanly anti-reformers. A great pile of licentious abominations is being burned, while Cruikshank's old friend Alderman Curtis, fatter than ever, stands with knife and fork in hand as if waiting

for something delicious to be cooked. On the right, Wellington disposes of *The Political House That Jack Built* on the end of his sword. On the left, the president of the association, Sir John Sewell (who had a withered leg), forks in *The Queen's Matrimonial Ladder*. This has a special point: both the Ladder and *Non Mi Ricordo* were prosecuted by the association. However, the indictments were thrown out by a grand jury; so were many others, including some against single caricatures; and the association dwindled away in ridicule.

A Slap at Slop could not ignore Castlereagh. The black-bordered picture dares to show him smilingly flogging a man by the method used when he was Chief Secretary in Dublin in 1798. A coffin is ready. Beneath this drawing Hone put: 'The printer has mislaid the manuscript belonging to this *cut*.' A year later, when Castlereagh was buried in Westminster Abbey (instead of at a crossroad with a stake through his heart, like humbler suicides) part of the crowd cheered as the hearse went in.

THE ROYAL EXTINGUISHER, OR THE KING OF BROBDINGNAG & THE LILLIPUTIANS,

7 April 1821

This must have been some consolation to George IV for the unkind things Cruikshank had done. The king holds a giant version of the extinguishers used to put out candles, and is about to trap a rabble of radicals and quench the 'sedition' firebrand held by Queen Caroline (who holds her '50,000 per Ann' moneybag). Some of the fleeing radicals are going to be caught by Lord Chancellor Eldon (left), a high Tory who was one of the king's favourite ministers. Sidmouth and Castlereagh (behind Eldon), Wellington (right background) and Liverpool are all delighted. The royal sun disperses clouds of discord; the queen is going into eclipse.

Cruikshank credited his brother Robert with a share in the design. It is an interesting example of how caricaturists found inspiration in the past. The brothers evidently had on their work-table a caricature done by their father in December 1795, 'The Royal Extinguisher or Gulliver Putting Out the Patriots of Lilliput!!!' It shows William Pitt similarly using an extinguisher at a time when Treason and Sedition Bills were being passed to silence an earlier generation of radicals.

AWAY FROM POLITICS

1821-34

Throughout the period from 'The Funeral Pile' to *A Slap at Slop*, George Cruikshank and his brother Robert were working on an entirely non-political monthly serial production, *Life in London* (see page 19). For George it was a first great success in depicting the drama and drollery of contemporary life in a style that was not caricature but was derived from it. Its success no doubt encouraged his turn away from political caricature in the 1820s; but so did his ambitions, his changing politics, and a decline in the caricature trade with a rise in the relative importance of cheap books and periodicals.

Both the *Life in London* plates reproduced here are from the July 1821 instalment. The first shows a cellar in Dyott Street, near St Giles's Church, Holborn, which was the night refuge of cadgers – people who survived by begging or semi-begging, some of them by pretending to be crippled. The title contains the first use in print of the word 'slums'. The three men-about-town, Corinthian Tom, Jerry Hawthorn and Logic the Oxonian, are 'masquerading it' in old clothes to visit the place. Tom, centre-stage chucking the chin of a ballad-singer, is based on George Cruikshank himself – though in this series he always makes himself taller than his actual five-foot-six, being a vain man. Jerry (Robert Cruikshank) is at the table, right, in green coat and a hat. Logic (Pierce Egan, author of *Life in London*) is beyond him, in round hat and glasses.

Some of Egan's description is worth quoting, complete with his italics: '*Peg*, the ballad-singer, all in tatters and covered with various-coloured rags, yet her pretty face did not escape the roving eye of Tom, upon her winking and leering her ogles at him and chaunting the ballad, ''Poverty's no sin'' in hopes to procure a new *fancy-man*.' Her ballads, printed on narrow strips, are in her basket.

Behind Tom a boy is filling a beer-pot. Next to him is an old negro.

'Massa Piebald, as they termed him, on account of his *black* mug and white *mop*, was *chaffing* the little *cove* that, as he had no *pins* to stand upon, he must have a *perch*; and . . . he proposed him for their chairman.' This dwarf is Little Jemmy, who became King of the Beggars in succession to Billy Waters, the one-legged negro fiddler who appeared in 'Landing the Treasures' a couple of years earlier and who now can be seen playing in his feathered hat and blond wig.

One false cripple is just arriving: 'Quarrelsome old *Suke*, who has been hobbling all the day on her *crutches* through the streets, now descends the ladder quickly to join the party, and is *blowing-up* her *ould man* for not taking hold of her crutches, ''as he knows she doesn't vant 'em now''.' Behind the stove, people are fighting with crutches and wooden legs 'till they are again wanted to cadge for the next day'; and 'the *peck* and *booze* is lying about in such lots that it would supply numerous poor families'.

Egan finishes: 'The whole plate is equal to any thing in Hogarth's collection; it may be examined again and again with delight.'

Only five years later, in a series called *The English Spy*, illustrated by Robert Cruikshank, it is stated that this Beggars' Club, with its 'notorious impostors, professional paupers, ballad-singers and blind fiddlers', is no more: 'The police have now disturbed their nightly orgies and the Mendicant Society ruined their *lucrative* calling. The long table, where the trenchers consisted of so many round holes turned out in the plank, and the knives, forks, spoons, candlesticks and fire-irons [were] *all chained* to their separate places, is no longer to be seen. The night-cellar yet exists, where the wretched obtain a temporary lodging and straw bed at twopence a head; but . . . scarce a vestige remains of the disgusting depravity of former times.'[129] Dickens and others were later to show that beggary was not so simply dealt with.

TOM AND JERRY 'MASQUERADING IT' AMONG THE CADGERS IN THE 'BACK SLUMS' IN THE HOLY LAND
July 1821

A WHISTLING SHOP. TOM AND JERRY VISITING LOGIC 'ON BOARD THE FLEET'
July 1821

'A Whistling Shop' takes Tom, Jerry and Logic a little higher in the social scale. Poor Logic has been confined to the Fleet Prison for debt, and Tom and Jerry are visiting him in a room where illicit drink may be bought and visitors received. A little boy standing beside his dejected father stares at the scene, just as Charles Dickens must have done when visiting his father in another prison, the Marshalsea, a couple of years later. Two men play cribbage, there is a fireplace, a prisoner enters carrying rackets: jail could be tolerable for some, before humanitarian reform imposed uniform cold degradation.

So many people cashed in on Tom and Jerry – in the theatre, in popular papers, in broadsides, on teatrays, snuffboxes, handkerchiefs and fans – that Cruikshank became bitter. When Egan, down on his luck about 1830, wrote to Cruikshank asking him to do a dozen sketches for some new project, he replied that if Egan's subject touched 'in the slightest degree upon the Tom & Jerry story' which 'has been run down by fools and spoil'd' he would 'have no heart to touch pencil upon it – indeed – everything as we have often said is attacked by the rasculy pirates.'[130]

A generation later the world of *Life in London* seemed an age away. Thackeray, writing in 1854, recalls some of the Cruikshank scenes, and says, 'The children of today, turning to their elders, may say, ''Grand-mamma, did you wear such a dress as that when you danced at Al-mack's? There was very little of it, grandmamma. Did grandpapa kill many watchmen when he was a young man, and frequent thieves, gin-shops, cock-fights and the ring before you married him? . . . He is very much changed. He seems a gentlemanly old boy enough now.''[131]

THE COMFORTS OF A CABRIOLET! OR THE ADVANTAGES OF DRIVING HOODWINK'D!!
March 1821

A multiple crash in or near Hyde Park. The newfangled cabriolets of 1821 (an import from France), with their 'hoodwink' tops, were not suitable for furious driving.

The first cabriolets for hire, with well-placed driver's seat, were plying in April 1823, and soon became known as cabs.

BACKSIDE & FRONT VIEW OF THE LADIES' FANCY-MAN, PADDY CAREY O'KILLUS, 20 July 1822

The statue erected at Hyde Park Corner in honour of Wellington and his soldiers – known from the start, incorrectly, as the Achilles Statue – was a source of mirth for several reasons. When it was unveiled on 14 July 1822 (not an accidental date, for it was made from captured Napoleonic guns), it was revealed as the first public nude statue in England. It had been paid for by subscriptions totalling £10,000 from the women of England. And Wellington was known not to have been valiantly faithful to his plain, dull wife: it was he who said a few years later, when the notorious Harriette Wilson suggested that he, like many others, could buy his way out of her memoirs, 'Publish and be damned!'

Cruikshank calls Wellington Paddy Carey O'Killus [Achilles] – and quotes some lines from a much-loved song, Paddy Carey, about a brawny Irishman who 'was loved by all the ladies'. Wellington himself, much caricatured, stands admiring the statue in the lefthand scene while a plump woman says, 'See, my ball o' wax! what we ladies *can raise* when we wish to put a man in mind of what he has done & we hope *will do again* when call'd for!!!' Most of the other remarks are also double-meaning. One woman makes a joke that would have remained topical for the next hundred years: 'I understand it is intended to represent His Grace after bathing in the Serpentine & defending himself from the attack of constables.'

GEORDIE & WILLIE 'KEEPING IT UP'–JOHNNY BULL PAYS THE PIPER!!

3 September 1822

George IV was so pleased with the welcome Dublin gave him that he sailed the next year to Scotland. At least he saw more of his realm than did his father, who never ventured further than Cheltenham.

Sir Walter Scott, George IV's favourite author, holder of a £3,000-a-year sinecure, helped to organize the festivities at Edinburgh. It was his odd notion to put lowland Scots into the kilt, which hitherto had been highland wear – banned, moreover, in living memory as the seditious dress of anti-Hanoverian Jacobites. Scott persuaded the Hanoverian George himself to wear the kilt (Stuart tartan), at a levee; and sure enough, the enormous red-nosed Alderman William Curtis, who had joined the royal jaunt – 'the boy for a bit of a jollification' – wore a kilt as well. His insignia of a turtle serves for a sporran; the sausages round his neck make him an alderman in chains (a phrase for a turkey with sausages that dates from the eighteenth century).

'Look at Sir William,' Hazlitt wrote the year before. '. . . He rolls about his unwieldy bulk in a sea of turtle-soup. How many haunches of venison does he carry on his back! He is larded with jobs and contracts; he is stuffed and swelled out with layers of bank-notes, and invitations to dinner!'[132] A lampoon on the Scottish trip has Curtis singing:

> My yacht, all can tell her:
> A mile off you may smell her.
> 'That's the *steam-boat* for me!' they all cry . . .
> She's like a rich dish
> Of ven'son or fish . . .[133]

The king has, suggestively, the largest possible sporran and he sings a snatch of Burns. The woman hiding her face with a fan may have been suggested by a song published at the time:

> With his tartan plaid and kilt so wide,
> The ladies blush who stand beside;
> And as he bows, behind each fan
> Exclaim, 'Oh, gallant Highlandman,
> Sing ho, the brawny Highlandman,
> The handy-dandy Highlandman!
> Oh, happy day when this way ran
> The English-Irish Highlandman!'[134]

THE BLUE DEVILS,

January 1823

The blue devils (later shortened to 'the blues') torment their victim with visions of disaster – bankruptcy, fire, tempest, bastardy, summonses (a beadle escorts three pregnant women) and death (a doctor is closely followed by a coffin-bearer); and urge him to suicide by pistol, razor and rope.

Cruikshank's preliminary ink and pencil study (much reduced, left) points up, by contrast, his over-working of the finished product – in later years a frequent weakness as his inspiration became uncertain.

JEALOUSY
November 1825

The jealous man has visions of a flashy guards officer wooing his love (left) and getting her to elope (right), watched by a smiling collusive constable. The man has been reading an anonymous letter – and Goethe's Werther. A dun presents a bill for £1,000; a pistol offers itself. On the mantel, the officer kills him in a duel. Cruikshank credits the design to his friend Alfred Forrester ('A. Crowquill'); who probably inspired 'The Blue Devils' as well.

THE SOLDIER AND HIS DOXY

These three etchings for Burns's *Jolly Beggars*, done in 1823, are among Cruikshank's first illustrations to a text in this intense, compressed style, which he was to employ a great deal in the next thirty years, but seldom with such effect. He read his Burns lovingly. The soldier and his doxy:

> First, neist the fire, in auld, red rags,
> Ane sat, weel brac'd wi' mealy bags
>   And knapsack a' in order;
> His doxy lay within his arm,
> Wi' usquebae an' blankets warm,
>   She blinket on her Sodger:
>
> An' aye he gies the tozie drab
>   The tither skelpan kiss,
> While she held up her greedy gab
>   Just like an aumous dish . . .

Lockhart, in the article quoted earlier, much admires this scene. 'The old fellow's face, you observe, is round, and drawn to a point at the nose; his eyes are almost quite shut; his firm lip projects about an inch beyond his pimpled proboscis . . . His three-cornered iron-bound hat is cocked half fiercely, half jauntily, on the right ear . . . And she! what a simper! what quiet luxury about her heavy eyelids, and that indescribable, ineffacable muzzle! The great toe of her right foot is curled up in an ecstasy of ''nothing loath'' – she shows, after all she has come through, a plump and juicy calf – her right hand is fumbling about his breastplate, and the left, half unconsciously, as it were, is fiddling about the tankard on the table there behind her.'[135]

THE TINKER AND THE FIDDLER

THE BALLADMONGER

Next is the 'pigmy scraper with his fiddle' whose delight in the widow of a 'gallant, braw John Highlandman' is invaded by a tinker:

> Her charms had struck a sturdy caird
>   As weel as poor gutscraper;
> He taks the fiddler by the beard
>   An' draws a roosty rapier –
> He swoor by a' was swearing worth
>   To speet him like a pliver
> Unless he wad from that time forth
>   Relinquish her for ever:
> Wi' ghastly e'e poor Tweedledee
>   Upon his hunkers bended
> And pray'd for grace wi' ruefu' face
>   An' so the quarrel ended.

The balladmonger, says Lockhart, 'is the best . . . the glory of the book': 'What a profound sense of the glorious felicity of whisky is manifested in this half-sleepy, half-enthusiastic, fat, bald, freckled, leering, squinting, gaping, roaring physiognomy.'[136]

> He, rising, rejoicing,
>   Between his two Debòrahs,
> Looks round him an' found them
>   Impatient for the chorus:
>
> *A fig for those by law protected!*
>   *Liberty's a glorious feast!*
> *Courts for cowards were erected,*
>   *Churches built to please the priest . . .*
>
> Life is all a variorum,
>   We regard not how it goes;
> Let them cant about decorum
>   Who have characters to lose . . .

FASHIONABLE LUXURY—OR A NEW-GENT AT MOTHER ----'S—WITH HIS FAVOURITE IRISH DICKY BIRDS
20 November 1824

Almost the last caricature with bawdy content by the now-married Cruikshank; and the man he exposes is made genial enough. He is thirty-six-year-old Lord Nugent, MP for Aylesbury, at a high-class brothel, Mother Wood's. His hat holds an essay 'on the *liberty* of the subject & *universal* suffrage' because he is a reformist Whig. The dicky-birds and the whiskey are Irish because Nugent, though an Englishman, held a title in the Irish peerage.

Cruikshank works here in the style of Gillray. He does not sign his name, but he makes a little joke: '*Miss Frances* (that is, Fanny) *Hill invt/Etched by A. Mac-Naughton*' – the latter being his churchy mother's family name.

OLD BUMBLEHEAD THE 18TH TRYING ON THE NAPOLEON BOOTS—
OR, PREPARING FOR THE SPANISH CAMPAIGN
17 February 1823

Cruikshank's fading interest in political caricature was revived briefly in 1823 by his distaste for the Holy Alliance. Louis XVIII was preparing to send an army into Spain to save Ferdinand VII in the tangled aftermath of an uprising against his absolutist rule. Louis talks of bear's grease because Tsar Alexander was supporting him. Poor Louis was indeed so gouty that he was often moved about in a wheeled chair. Whigs in England were prophesying that the French would meet disaster in Spain and Louis might lose his throne—which is why Napoleon's twelve-year-old son is shown reaching for the crown, and why a red-bonneted guillotine arises in the distance. The boy wears Napoleon's Chasseur uniform.

But the French marched and succeeded with hardly a battle.

KEEN-ISH SPORT IN COX'S COURT!! OR SYMPTOMS OF CRIM. CON. IN DRURY LANE
May 1824

As a young enthusiast for the theatre, Cruikshank had known Edmund Kean before he became the star of Drury Lane during the Regency; but that did not stop Cruikshank from caricaturing him (anonymously) when he became involved in a scandal. The woman is Mrs Charlotte Cox, whose well-horned husband was an alderman and gold dealer – hence Kean's phrase about his love being 'pure as refined gold'.

'Crim. con.' was the current abbreviation for the legal term for adultery, criminal conversation. Symptoms indeed: Cox sued and got £800 damages. Kean's acting was already suffering from his drinking (note the brandy bottle), and now his audiences turned hostile.

[114]

THE ADVANTAGES OF TRAVEL, OR 'A LITTLE LEARNING IS A DANGEROUS THING'–PLATE 1

Comment se porte mon ami? – Moi, I am jost come from de England. – Aha, you vas jost come from de England! Den how you like de bif? Le bif roti is charmant à Londres! – Yase, dat is vrai, bote je prefare le rum-tek! – Le rum-tek! Vat is de rum-tek? – Voyez-vous, it is toujours de bif-tek, mais, bote, day call it rum-tek ba-cause day pote de *rum* in de sauce.

14 June 1824

Cruikshank never condescended to take a trip to Paris, but he etched many French scenes with the help of other men's sketches and of his observation of French people in London. The pair of jokes on this page and the next were the invention of his friend John Parry. Tourists have not changed much: getting things slightly wrong, and not wanting to admit ignorance.

How many national contrasts survive? The French are more elegant: note the contrasted waiters in particular. The Frenchmen's trousers are in the latest mode; the lefthand Englishman in Plate 2 is a rumpled John Bullish mess, with two bundles adding to his bulk in a most ungentlemanlike way. The passing Englishwoman contrives to show a lot of

ankle – which dates her, to judge by the Frenchwoman in Plate 1. Umbrellas have come in; was it bad form to lean on one?

John Bullock's eating house, with its 'genteel dining rooms upstairs' and its unenticing waiter, boasts of nothing but à-la-mode beef, hams and tongues. A patisserie next-door gives hot competition with 'Diner à la carte' and 'Déjeuner à la fourchette' as well as jellies and ices. The Paris restaurant in Plate 1 has been influenced already by the tourist trade: 'Ici on parle l'anglois', and welch rabbit and biftek are offered. We must not look for an English eating house in Paris, of course. But in one thing London is ahead: it has a pavement for pedestrians.

[115]

THE ADVANTAGES OF TRAVEL, OR 'A LITTLE LEARNING IS A DANGEROUS THING'–PLATE 2
14 June 1824

Ah, Jack, how are ye? – Devilish well, just crossed the water, been to Paris! – Well, and how did ye like the cooking? – Confounded good, 'pon my soul. Liked their harrico blong best. – What's harrico blong? – What's harrico blong! Why, you know what harrico is, don't ye? – To be sure! It's mutton chops and carrots and turnips, with wedgables. – Very well, then. *That's it*. And Blong you know's the name o' the first cook as made it. – Oh, aye, so it is. I remember now! !

MONSTROSITIES OF 1825 – & 6
10 February 1826

The journalist and publisher Charles Knight, writing his reminiscences in 1864, looked at his caricature collection and said: 'As for costume – what can be more trustworthy than these gaudily-coloured extravagancies? The bonnet stretching over the *manches à gigot* like a vast umbrella – the waist compressed into stays that sever the fair one's body into two portions wasp-like – the mountains of ribbon at top, and the acres of flounces below . . . The gentleman . . . is reduced to the smallest possible dimensions by his own stays, over which the closely-fitting coat is buttoned with the utmost exertion of the valet's strength . . . How these creatures move is not easy to comprehend . . . These were the days when whiskers came in – timid precursors of the ample beard.'[137]

Cruikshank probably went to Hyde Park on a Sunday to do his sketches (which survive) for this. *The English Spy* says:

> In cockney land, the seventh day
> Is famous for a grand display
> Of modes, of finery and dress
> Of cit, west-ender and *noblesse,*
> Who in Hyde Park crowd like a fair
> To stare, and lounge, and take the air,
> Or ride or drive, or walk and chat
> On fashions, scandal and all that.[138]

SAILORS CAROUSING

Cruikshank's only military experience was with a part-time volunteer unit, the Loyal North Britons, towards the end of the Napoleonic wars; and then many years later as an officer in the 48th Middlesex Rifle Volunteers. But as a boy he had wanted to go to sea (as his brother Robert did for a spell), and he liked depicting the old-fashioned British seadog. These are three of the twelve etchings he did for a book of naval reminiscences, *Greenwich Hospital*, in 1825. The author, Captain Matthew Barker, guided him and drew some sketches to ensure accuracy, so we have here some reliable glimpses of the navy that then ruled the waves.

The book is mainly in the words of veterans living out their days at Greenwich. This is the passage Cruikshank followed in 'Sailors Carousing': 'The evening was rattled away in jollity and punch. Ah, them were the times, messmates! I thinks I sees 'em all now jigging away, while the fiddlers scraped the cat-gut, and the grog flowed in purly streams, and the volumes of smoke rolled their columns to the ceiling.' Times are changing: 'I understands they are going to shorten the allowance in the navy; but mark my words – 't won't do. They may just as well take away Jack's life at once as to go for to stop his grog . . . Ay, ay, they may talk of their tea and slop, but 't won't do, I say, and so they'll find it.'

Here again we have an affectionate picture of humble pleasures; and in the middle of it Cruikshank puts himself – the dancer in blue jacket and yellow hat. Is the girl his first wife?

SAILORS ON A CRUISE

The sailors 'on a cruise' belong to a famous ship, *Arethusa*: her flag is lashed to the coach. 'That was the ship, she was one of the fleetest of the fleet – sailed like a witch, sat down on the water like a duck. Why, she could do anything but speak.' The sailors are celebrating at Plymouth on their return from capturing a French ship. Their prize-money went merrily: 'Five on 'em bought a coach, horses and all, and then hired the coachman for three days to drive about – but all hands kept upon deck, and left the inside empty; for what was the use of skulking under hatches in fine weather? So, d'ye see, they stowed the craft well with grog and 'bacca – got all snug, with a fiddler and an organ-grinder abaft, and carried on between Plymouth and Dock during the whole time they stopped on shore. Ah, them were the days! when a sailor had no trouble getting rid of his money; but now he can't gather as much as would jingle upon a tombstone.'[139]

This etching of 1799, published by Laurie & Whittle and almost certainly done by Isaac Cruikshank, looks as if it served as inspiration for George's 'Sailors on a Cruise'. It is entitled 'True Blue: The Jolly Tars of Old England, or All Alive at Portsmouth.'

CROSSING THE LINE

'Crossing the Line' gives a lively picture of the old rumbustious ceremony on crossing the equator. The victim in the tub is getting a tar-brush in the face while a bucket of sea-water is poured on him through a funnel. Another blindfold victim is being carried in, right; behind him, the ship's captain hands a drink to a sailor dressed as Neptune's consort.

BEAUTIES OF BRIGHTON
1 March 1826

This promenade past George IV's fantastical Brighton Pavilion (somewhat exaggerated) was developed by Cruikshank from a drawing by his friend Alfred Forrester – who is walking into the scene, left, with his two brothers.

The portly man beneath the onion dome is the Duke of York, who no longer looks hearty, and was to die of dropsy the following year, 1827, enormously in debt. Behind the veiled woman is John Liston, comedian, a favourite of George IV and then at the height of his fame in the character Paul Pry. The fat man in black, walking to the right, is Nathan Rothschild the banker, with his wife in an assertive hat. Far right, in feathered hat, Harriet Coutts (née Harriet Mellon, actress), vastly rich widow of Thomas Coutts the banker; the following year she restored the fortunes of the Duke of St Albans by marrying him. Entering right, one of the age's great survivors, Talleyrand (a dozen years before, Cruik-

shank was merrily picturing his clubfoot; now he tactfully leaves it out of the picture).

In the foreground, the too, too fashionable young man nicely counterpoints the shape of the woman facing him. His hair hangs about his ears; and he wears ear-rings.

The English Spy complains that all sorts of people now come down from London (with five changes of horses, the coach took a little over five hours): 'You have the felicity to meet your tailor in his tandem, your shoemaker in his fly, and your wine-merchant with his bit of blood, his girl and tilbury, making a greater *splash* than yourself.' But nobody makes a greater splash than Harriet Coutts: 'The great star of attraction is the rich banker's widow . . . eclipsing in splendid equipages and attendants an eastern nabob, or royalty itself.'[140]

DOVER COACH – 5 O'CLOCK – MORNING
25 August 1826

The pleasures of travel, 1826. Again Alfred Forrester is the artist.

COVETIVENESS

LANGUAGE

Two of the thirty-three large and small designs, mainly anecdotal or joky, in Cruikshank's first attempt at independent publishing, in August 1826, *Phrenological Illustrations* (see page 21).

'Covetiveness' nicely contrasts the plodding self-important gentleman and the intent silent work of the pickpocketing team. The larger thief's coat pocket is already bulging with loot. The picture precedes Cruikshank's work for *Oliver Twist* by eleven years.

'Language!' is a scene at Billingsgate fish-market beside the Thames, where strong words had been proverbial at least since the seventeenth century.

TIME CALLED & TIME COME

Cruikshank's second independent publication, *Illustrations of Time*, came out in May 1827, and was given an admiring review the following month in *Blackwood's* by 'Christopher North' (Professor John Wilson). His words are the best commentary on the prizefight:

'Conspicuous in the middle of the picture stands the Time-Keeper, with his tatler in his hand – bawling the monosyllable. To his left . . . lies on his back, with his face up to heaven, the man of the flash side – say Jem Ward – in a state of innocence. His daylights are darkened, and something more than slumber has sealed up his eyes, which have been lanced in vain. In vain, too, does his strong-lunged second roar into his ear. To him, it is like a faint and far-off echo – or perhaps he hears it not at all . . . His bottle-holder, on one knee, and with one fist half-angrily clenched, seems to upraid him for being past the restoration of the water of life. A Jew kneels over him in despair, mutter-

ing and moaning about his 'monish' – while a sporting surgeon feels the feeble pulse . . . and a great big hulking disconsolate Cockney, such a one as always appertains to the flash side, half swell and half gull, can with difficulty believe his heyes . . . And there, close to the ninny's elbow, is that familiar, Bill Richmond, the Lily-white [a noted boxer] . . . his ogles leering with a knavish I've-neither-lost-nor-won hedgingish expression . . . Five more finished reprobates you will rarely see in a pyramidal group, and should the man die they will be all lagged together . . .

'But look at his opponent! Second and bottle-holder lift him like a log from the sod . . . his face is indistinguishable in mouth, nose or eyes – but he staggers up to the scratch like a drunkard, and then, as deaf to time as his antagonist, falls down with a squelch – thirteen stone – bating a few pounds of sweat and blood.'

BEHIND TIME

Christopher North also admired 'Behind Time':

'We absolutely hear him groan when Mr Tapstave, the boniface, says to his glaring question, "Coach sir!! The coach has been gone sir, about three-quarters of an hour sir – they start sir, to their time sir, to a minute sir!" What a face! . . . The coach runs but once a week, and Taffy and his spouse must wait till next Tuesday . . . No wonder he is breathless and aghast, for he is laden with portmanteau, and travelling-bag, and bundle, and umbrella, and great-coat, and shawls, and pelisses . . . With band-box and child, his better half is seen flying under a load of fat through the market-place . . . Hapless pair! What could you have been about since six o'clock this morning, when you rose?'[141]

William Clarke takes the innkeeper as an example of Cruikshank's talent for conveying a man's character: 'The fat knock-kneed fellow, with his eyes half-closed . . . is a publican who decidedly commenced his career as a potboy . . . He never had a good night's rest in his life. He takes a nap in the skittle-ground every fine afternoon . . . He is not fat – he is blown out like a bad shoulder of veal . . . His wife thrashed him the night before last, because *she* broke a cracked coffee-cup . . . The miserable man who is "behind time" has been so all his life.'[142]

Cruikshank's third private venture, *Scraps and Sketches* (20 May 1828), consists like the first two of six large folio sheets of etchings, bound together; but there is no single theme.

'HOUSE OF INDUSTRY'

IGNORANCE IS BLISS

Although Cruikshank is now avoiding political controversy, in 'House of Industry' he puts in a word for the unregarded workman. The cobbler's wife and three children all help him, but he doubts if he can afford meat two Sundays in a row (they have none on weekdays). Cruikshank accompanies the drawing with the words of an old song, 'A cobbler there was and he lived in a stall/Which served him for parlour and kitchen and hall.' The phrase 'House of Industry' alludes to the workplaces then being discussed for paupers.

'Ignorance is Bliss', with its overfed servants and bloated dog at the door of a great town house, made a lasting impression. Eighteen years later, John Leech did a political version in *Punch* with dialogue which unhappily is still not outdated: Robert Peel – 'What is to be done with Ireland, John?' Lord John Russell – 'I'm sure I don't know.'

THE AGE OF INTELLECT

PRACTISING AT THE BAR

From the same issue of *Scraps and Sketches*, jokes about a new trend and about a longstanding cause of complaint.

The 1820s brought a great growth of movements for popular education. There was much talk of the March of Intellect. A university not controlled by the Church of England – a daring innovation – was founded in London. Magazines packed with general knowledge were launched; some of them with the aim of diverting the common people from radical reading. Superior people mocked the rage for learning, and in 'The Age of Intellect' Cruikshank joins in the mockery. Geometry, chemistry, Shakespeare, Bacon, Milton, Locke, Hume and Gibbon are among the texts being studied by the little girl advising grandma on egg-sucking.

'Practising at the Bar' offers two laughs: in its title, and in the burglar's remark about the snoring watchman. It was the following year that Peel organized the New Police.

Lady Dashington finds that the newest fashion in hats is too much for a St James's Park gateway. A guardsman helps another lady solve the problem.

LADY DASHINGTON'S BONNET STOPS THE WAY!

THE GIN SHOP
1 November 1829

This is Cruikshank's first out-and-out anti-drink print – eighteen years before he took the teetotal pledge and became a constant campaigner for the cause. The gin-drinking group at the bar, including two children and a baby, stand within a man-trap ('gin' in the title also means a trap). The barmaid is a masked skeleton. Death (a night-watchman, with hourglass instead of lantern) waits confidently. Labels at the corners of the design give four destinations for drunkards.

Some elements of the picture are derived from a scene in Rowlandson's *English Dance of Death*, 1815. Rowlandson has a skeleton pouring vitriol and aqua fortis into the gin barrels. Cruikshank speaks of aqua-fortis in some verses beneath his design:

Now, oh dear, how shocking the thought is,
They makes the gin from aqua fortis:
They do it on purpose, folks' lives to shorten
And tickets it up at two-pence a quartern.

IS THE LABOURER WORTHY OF HIS HIRE?

1 November 1829

A MAN 'WITH ALL HIS LITTLE COMFORTS ABOUT HIM'

February 1831

This is from a second *Scraps and Sketches* collection (as is 'The Gin shop').

The astonished maidservant would not be getting a guinea a month from her well-to-do mistress.

In his third *Scraps and Sketches*, from which this comes, Cruikshank indulges in a growing number of sad visual puns and whimsical variations on comical everyday objects such as bellows. But in this little etching he achieves an uneasy balance between sentiment, realism and the comic. Perhaps the Cruikshank who understood the poor and sometimes wished for the simple life was also thinking here of the childlessness of his own household.

'JUST ROOM FOR THREE INSIDES, SIR'
February 1831

The horses are alarmed: 'What, all fat? Really this is too bad.' Their friend Martin is Richard Martin, the MP who in 1822 achieved the first legislation against cruelty to animals.

Cruikshank's friend William Clarke has a comic coaching scene in his periodical *The Cigar*, 1825. A fat citizen ('only 17 stone 6, jockey weight') keeps a diary of a trip to Dover: 'Inside crammed, and all five comfortable, having made up their minds that I, the sixth, shouldn't come to time. General discomfiture at my large appearance! . . . Bustle, terror, ejaculation – "Balance of power!" – "Six inside, too many by one!" – "Rather corpulent!" . . . Squeezed like a jelly bag, oozing at all pores – sullen – silent – looked mysterious. Hints and surmises by passengers . . . Says I, "Sir," with gravity, "Sir, I am a pickpocket, much at your service." Violent consternation! Seat more easy by half . . . Coach changed horses – man on my right got out – "Ride on the roof, rather sick, very full . . ." Comfortable, easy as arm-chair . . .'[143]

LONDON GOING OUT OF TOWN – OR THE MARCH OF BRICKS & MORTAR
1 November 1829

Cruikshank had only to look out of the western windows of his Myddelton Terrace house in 1829 to see the march of bricks and mortar up the slope towards him, as well as some of the kilns that were making the bricks. The scene in 'London Going out of Town', however, is a geographical composite, bringing in St Paul's, in reality a mile and a half south of where new houses were chasing the sheep, cows, haycocks and trees from the green fields of Islington. In the other direction, the heights of Hampstead lay beyond miles of farmland dotted with villages; but Hampstead Heath was indeed in danger, for the Lord of the Manor, Sir Thomas Wilson, was trying to push through a Bill to enclose it.

Cruikshank's friend William Hone shared his sorrow at the great growth of London. In 1825 Hone wrote in his *Every-Day Book* about the view from Canonbury Tower (a mile beyond where Cruikshank lived): 'The eye shrunk from the wide havoc below. Where new buildings had not covered the sward, it was embowelling for bricks, and kilns emitted flickering fire and sulphurous stench. Surely the dominion of the brick-and-mortar king will have no end.'[144] It was the same further west. *The English Spy* says: 'At the foot of Primrose-hill we are amazed by coming upon a large complication of streets . . . The rustic and primeval meadows of Kilburn are also filling with raw buildings and incipient roads; to say nothing of the charming neighbourhood of St John's Wood Farm.'[145]

[131]

THE HORSES 'GOING TO THE DOGS'
1 November 1829

Again, Cruikshank is unhappy about a new development. The dogs are looking forward to a glut of horse-meat. The steam carriage is not his fantasy: four months earlier, the inventor Goldsworthy Gurney ran one from London to Bath and back at fifteen miles an hour. A Gloucester-Cheltenham service ran for three months in 1831, until it was stopped by prohibitory tolls. Then the coming of the railways settled the argument for sixty years.

PUFFING A GRATE SINGER
February 1831

The pair of sketches above are the more bearable of a whole sheet of whimsies about bellows in Cruikshank's third *Scraps and Sketches*. They prove at least that such puns were thought of before the Victorians.

NOBODY DESIRES THE PAINTER TO MAKE HIM AS UGLY AND AS RIDICULOUS AS POSSIBLE
February 1831

Here is Cruikshank in 1831 (when he was doing some oil painting), putting himself into a joke with the torso-less Nobody character who had been a caricature stock-in-trade for more than two hundred years. For once, Cruikshank is willing to draw himself as the short man he was.

SWEEPING MEASURES, OR MAKING A CLEAN HOUSE
23 March 1831

This is one of the two political caricatures that were all that Cruikshank could be persuaded to do during the passionate conflict over reform of 1830–2; a period from which 1,165 political caricatures survive in the British Museum collection.

Two days before 'Sweeping Measures', the same printshop, Knight's of Sweeting's Alley, published Cruikshank's 'The System that Works so Well' – a title mocking the phrase used by people who did not want it changed. That caricature was a variation on a theme that Cruikshank had used twenty years before in 'State Miners' and again in 'Economic Humbug' – the organized flow of John Bull's money into the hands of undeserving parasites. 'Sweeping Measures', too, is hardly original. The new broom (wielded here by Lord John Russell) had been used in caricatures when Wellington's Tory government was swept from

power in 1830. The rotten-borough creatures protesting in their cloud of dust all use phrases that were being repeated on the Tory side: 'This is not a reform, this is a revolution . . . You will destroy our Constitution . . . The king's crown is in danger!'

It is noticeable how much less savage Cruikshank has become. There had been a change of tone in the caricature trade, it is true; but the reform fight brought out all the old virulence in other caricaturists. And the public was given a direct reminder of the Cruikshank of ten years before: a series of pamphlets published by a radical journalist, William Carpenter, used dozens of his wood engravings, pirated from *The Political House That Jack Built, The Political Showman* and elsewhere.

SALUS POPULI SUPREMA LEX

February/March 1832

The reluctant satirist lends his talent for another sort of reform. The man enthroned on a close-stool in the middle of the Thames, with a chamberpot for crown, is John Edwards, owner of a company that supplied the borough of Southwark with its water. In 1828 an official report said that the water, 'if water it can be called,' came from 'the very spot in the Thames . . . at which the great common sewers emerge'. Now it is February 1832; cholera has just arrived in London by way of Sunderland to concentrate people's minds on hygiene; and Edwards is pumping away the same as ever (the chimneys of his pumping-house can be seen on the right).

The broadside illustrated by this etching calls Edwards 'Water-King of Southwark, Sovereign of the Scented Streams . . . Protector of the Confederation of the (U)Rhine . . . Warden of the Sink Ports', and a number of other filthy things. He gives a Royal Address in verse in which he says people get rid of 'all things that are dirty' down one hundred and thirty sewers into the river –

And should they be touched with the Sunderland gripes
The balmy effects of their stomachs and tripes
Are infallibly destined to roll through the pipes
    By which I replenish your houses.

. . . Let not Reform, though she daily grows stronger,
Decree that no borough shall rot any longer;
Still buy putrefaction of me, the old monger,
    And there yet shall be one Rotten Borough.

[135]

TELL TALE
September 1832

Most of Cruikshank's fourth *Scraps and Sketches* collection, which he published from his Myddelton Terrace address in 1832, suggests that he was finding it harder than ever to create ideas on his own. There is a sheet of visual puns about fish; a sheet of grotesque fashions; an attack on the licentiousness of Bartholomew Fair in Smithfield; a moral diptych of men boozing in an alehouse and a wife and baby languishing at home.

'Tell Tale', the centrepiece of a sheet of jokes on the word 'tail', has some point. Pigtails, over-enthusiastically made, could be almost as distressing as this. The victim is a Marine – a traditional butt of the ship's crew.

THE PILLARS OF A GIN SHOP
15 August 1833

In 1833 Cruikshank began a new series, *My Sketch Book* – still of large folio etched sheets bound together (two shillings and sixpence plain, three-and-six coloured for six sheets), but published 'for the artist' by a Fleet Street bookseller, Charles Tilt, with whom he was to be associated for many years. The medley of facetious and didactic items continues.

In this further attack on gin, Cruikshank shows, like Dickens, great sympathy for the children: the little crying girl and the ragged boy staring in rigid despair. There is a play, of course, on the ornate pillars of the house and the drinkers who can scarcely support themselves.

MOST APPROVED METHOD OF PULLING A FELLOW'S NOSE
(AS PRACTISED BY ST DUNSTAN)
August 1834

This portrait of Cruikshank in combative mood, rising forty-two and almost halfway through his life, can fittingly close this part of his story. It is the centrepiece of a sheet of vignettes about noses. The man he is dealing with, by the fire-tongs method which St Dunstan said he used on the devil, is a publisher named Kidd who had been pirating his work.

In these later years Cruikshank was often involved in quarrels, and not always with such good reason. Though generally good company, he could be touchy and abrupt. In 1841, the book *Portraits of Public Characters* tries to put it diplomatically: 'The ludicrous and extra-ordinary fancies with which his mind is constantly teeming often impart a sort of wildness to his look and peculiarity to his manner, which would suffice to frighten from his presence those unacquainted with him.' [146] He made mock of this, however, in *George Cruikshank's Omnibus*; and as for the book's suggestion that he easily vanquishes blustering, abusive cabmen ('. . . he darts a look at them which, in two cases out of three, has the effect of reducing them to a state of tolerable civility', and failing that, he finishes them off with 'a few indignant, vehement words'), Cruikshank says disarmingly: 'It so happens that I have never had a dispute with a cabman in my life . . . and frequently, by the exercise of a generous forgetfulness, make them a present of an

umbrella, a pair of gloves or a handkerchief. At times I have gone so far as to leave them a few sketches.' [147]

Another of his qualities, his vanity, is described by the publisher Henry Vizetelly, who first knew Cruikshank in 1835 when he was working with Vizetelly's father: 'One was not long in discovering how conceited the clever artist was in regard to his personal appearance, for he stealthily eyed himself in the glass on every available opportunity. He had been in the habit of picturing himself as a buck in his youth, and was still a bit of a fop, kept his hair well oiled and his whiskers punc-tiliously brushed, and was natty in his dress . . . He never depicted himself under a ridiculous aspect . . . he presented the public with a series of flattering self-likenesses.' [148]

It can be seen in the present self-likeness that he is brushing his hair forward to conceal frontal baldness. As the years passed, this concealing hair became longer and wilder, and his whiskers became wild too. The hair and the artist's piercing eyes are mentioned in an affectionate portrait by Charles Dickens in *Martin Chuzzlewit*, 1848. Mrs Gamp talking: '. . . a gentleman with a large shirt collar, and a hook nose, and a eye like one of Mr Sweedlepipes's hawks, and long locks of hair, and whiskers that I wouldn't have no lady as I was engaged to meet sud-denly a-turning a corner for any sum of money you could offer me.'

Geo: Cruikshank

NOTES

1 *Art Journal*, February 1863, p. 25.
2 For family dates and addresses see Appendix.
3 Aspinall, Arthur, *The Correspondence of George Prince of Wales,* 1963–71, II, p. 287.
4 Aspinall, *Correspondence*, II, pp. 298–303.
5 'The Gradual Abolition of the Slave Trade, or Leaving off Sugar by Degrees', 15 April 1792. For the content of other caricatures of this and later periods, consult the George catalogue (see Bibliography).
6 Graves, Algernon, *The Royal Academy of Arts: A Complete Dictionary of Contributors . . . ,* 1905.
7 Item 1974 U 1831 among Isaac Cruikshank sketches, British Museum.
8 Jerrold, Blanchard, *The Life of George Cruikshank*, 1882, I, p. 27.
9 Berkeley, Grantley F., *My Life and Recollections*, 1860, IV, p. 133. Berkeley himself did caricatures for Thomas McLean, the Haymarket printseller, and was paid for them.
10 This remark, often quoted, was first recorded by 'Cuthbert Bede' (Edward Bradley) in his 'Personal Recollections of George Cruikshank' in *The London Figaro*, 13 February to 13 March 1878. I have not been able to trace copies of this weekly.
11 See Wark, Robert R., *Isaac Cruikshank's Drawings for Drolls*, Huntington Library, San Marino, California, 1968.
12 *Laurie and Whittle's Catalogue of New and Interesting Prints*, 1795, p. 95. It lists 152 drolls, with 'new ones continually adding'; as well as thousands of other prints: 'landscapes; historical, sentimental and humorous; large sea pieces; wild beasts, race horses, hunting; scripture pieces; theatrical; portraits,' etc.
13 'A Meeting of Creditors', 3 April 1795.
14 *Fraser's Magazine*, August 1833, p. 190 (article by William Maginn, with portrait of George Cruikshank by Daniel Maclise).

15 Reid, George William, *A Descriptive Catalogue of the Works of George Cruikshank,* 1871, I, p. v.
16 Burke, Joseph, *Hogarth, The Analysis of Beauty*, 1955, p. 206.
17 Victoria & Albert Museum, manuscript note on item 9817.
18 Jerrold, *Life of Cruikshank*, I, p. 27.
19 Note by George Cruikshank on a caricature by his father, Sons of Friendship; quoted in catalogue of Francis Edwards Ltd, London, 1907.
20 *The Georgian Era* (publisher Vizetelly & Branston), 1834, IV, pp. 226–7.
21 Manuscript owned by David Borowitz, Chicago; written March 1860 for *Dictionary of Contemporary Biography*, 1861, which used an edited version.
22 *Monthly Magazine*, February 1833, 'Life and Genius of George Cruikshank', p. 140.
23 *George Cruikshank's Omnibus*, 1842, 'My Portrait', pp. 2–3.
24 *The Scourge*, August 1811, p. 94.
25 *Town Talk*, 23 November 1811, p. 34.
26 *The Scourge*, January 1812, p. 34.
27 *The Scourge*, September 1811, p. 207.
28 'The Fashionable Lady: Sung by Mr Grimaldi at Sadler's Wells', in *The Pride of Albion* (songbook), c. 1809.
29 *The Busy Body*, June 1816, p. 176.
30 Royal Archives, Manuscript 27094 et seq.
31 *Blackwood's Magazine*, July 1823, p. 18.
32 *The Meteor*, November 1813 (Bodleian).
33 *Monthly Magazine*, February 1833, p. 141.
34 Jerrold, *Life of Cruikshank*, I, p. 31.
35 British Museum, Prints & Drawings, item 1974 U 1847.
36 Jerrold, *Life of Cruikshank*, I, p. 36.
37 *George Cruikshank's Omnibus*, 1842, p. 28.
38 Hackwood, Frederick M., *William Hone: His Life and Times*, 1912, p. 34.
39 Todd, William B., *A Dictionary of Printers*, 1972.
40 British Museum Manuscript Add. 40120, ff. 91–2.

41 Hackwood, *William Hone*, p. 220.
42 Knight, Charles, *Passages of a Working Life*, 1864, I, pp. 245–6.
43 Royal Archives, Manuscript 51382a.
44 *The Loyalist's Magazine Complete*, 'presented to His Majesty at the Levee, February 22, 1821,' pp. 233–4.
45 *Slop's Shave at a Broken Hone*, 1820, p. 12.
46 Bodleian Manuscript Douce d.23, f. 234v.
47 Hone, William, *Aspersions Answered* (dated 1824, revised 1827), p. 49.
48 *The Radical Chiefs: A Mock Heroic Poem*, 1821, pp. 11–12.
49 Clarke, William, *The Cigar*, 1828 (first published 1825), II, p. 242 (Bodleian).
50 Cohn, Albert M., *George Cruikshank: A Catalogue Raisonné of the Work Executed during the Years 1806–1877*, 1924, p. xiii.
51 British Museum Manuscript Add. 41071, f. 5.
52 Hone, *Facetiae and Miscellanies*, 1827, pp. v–vi (written 1822).
53 Hackwood, *William Hone*, p. 190.
54 Idem.
55 *Tom and Jerry*, J. C. Hotten reissue, 1870, p. 13.
56 *The Georgian Era*, p. 228.
57 Bates, William, *George Cruikshank: The Artist, the Humorist and the Man*, 1879, p. 23.
58 *The Songs, Parodies, etc. introduced in the New Pedestrian-Equestrian Extravaganza* [etc], 1822.
59 Register of deaths, St Catherine's House, London; bill of Cooksey, undertaker (the firm survives in Amwell Street), in Bodleian, John Johnson Collection, George Cruikshank Box 2 (unindexed); *Monthly Magazine*, February 1833, p. 135.
60 Victoria & Albert, 10033 I.
61 British Library, Dex 315, Box IV (unindexed).
62 Collection of Ronald Searle.
63 Jerrold, *Life of Cruikshank*, II, p. 52.
64 Vizetelly, Henry, *Glances Back Through Seventy Years*, 1893, I, p. 105.

65 Register of deaths.

66 *Blackwood's Magazine*, July 1823, 'Lectures on the Fine Arts: No. 1, On George Cruikshank', pp. 18–20, 23.

67 *The Every-Day Book*, 1826 (reissued 1831, 1838, 1841, etc), II, col. 1121–7.

68 Cromwell, Thomas, *History and Description of the Parish of Clerkenwell*, 1828, p. 320.

69 *The Every-Day Book*, 1825, I, col. 877.

70 *Monthly Magazine*, February 1833, pp. 132–3.

71 *Notes & Queries*, 15 June 1878.

72 *The Annals of Sporting and Fancy Gazette*, July 1822, A Visit to the Fives Court, plate following p. 116.

73 *Monthly Magazine*, February 1833, p. 146.

74 *Fraser's Magazine*, August 1833, p. 190.

75 *Portraits of Public Characters*, 1841, II, p. 242.

76 *Fraser's Magazine*, August 1833, p. 190.

77 *Monthly Magazine*, February 1833, p. 146.

78 Catalogue of E. Foster & Son's auction, 13–16 July 1835, British Museum, Prints & Drawings.

79 Sold after his death, Christie's, 15 May 1878, 19 guineas, to 'Harvey' (presumably Francis Harvey, printseller, St James's St, for whom George Cruikshank engraved a trade card). Where is it now?

80 *Westminster Review*, June 1840, p. 6.

81 Ibid., p. 5.

82 *Quarterly Review*, December 1854, pp. 79, 80.

83 Manuscript of David Borowitz (see note 21).

84 Sala, George Augustus, *The Life and Adventures of . . .*, 1895, I, p. 206.

85 Bodleian, Frith. a. 13.

86 The 'Dear Little Darling', in 1809 songbook, *Joe Grim's Delight*.

87 Bickley, Francis, ed., *The Diaries of Sylvester Douglas, Lord Glenbervie*, 1928, II, p. 5.

88 *Lord Granville Leveson Gower: Private Correspondence 1781 to 1821*, 1916, II, p. 429.

89 *The Satirist*, May 1812, p. 381.

90 *The Satirist*, March 1812, 172–3, p. 206.

91 Aspinall, Arthur, *The Letters of King George IV, 1812–1830*, 1938, I, p. 419.

92 Gronow, Rees, *The Reminiscences and Recollections of Captain Gronow*, 1889, II, 4.

93 Ibid., I, p. 285.

94 *The Greville Memoirs 1814–1860*, ed. Lytton Strachey and R. Fulford, 1938, I, p. 4; *Glenbervie*, II, p. 127; Moore, Thomas, 'Parody of a Celebrated Letter'; Leveson Gower correspondence, II, p. 426.

95 British Museum Manuscript Eg. 3262, f. 34v, f. 38.

96 *The Scourge*, October 1813.

97 Moore, Thomas, *Intercepted Letters*, 1814, p. 57 (first published March 1812).

98 *Metropolitan Grievances*, By One Who Thinks for Himself, 1812, p. 78.

99 *The Scourge*, July 1812, pp. 80, 81.

100 *Fashion*, 1817, p. 20.

101 *The Busy Body*, June 1816, p. 177.

102 *Fashion*, p. 83, 86.

103 Bodleian Manuscript Douce e. 29, f. 33v.

104 Aspinall, *Letters of King George IV*, I, 15 March 1816.

105 Leveson Gower Correspondence, II, p.356.

106 Gronow, *Reminiscences*, I, p. 288.

107 *Hunting for the Heir ! ! ! The R---l H-mb-gs*, by Peter Pindar, Esq.

108 *Monthly Magazine*, February 1833, p. 141 (originally in *The Cigar*, 1825).

109 *The Fudge Family In Paris*, 1818.

110 *The Ton*, 1819, illustrated by George Cruikshank.

111 Luttrell, Henry, *Letters to Julia*, 1822, pp. 42, 43, 47.

112 Gronow, *Reminiscences*, I, p. 227.

113 *The Free-born Englishman deprived of his Seven Senses by the Operation of the Six New Acts of the Boroughmongers*, by Geoffrey Gag-'em-all (with George Cruikshank frontispiece).

114 Hazlitt, William, *The Complete Works*, 1934, VII, p. 286.

115 *The Real or Constitutional House that Jack Built*, 1819.

116 Victoria & Albert, 9503A/H: erased but decipherable. George Cruikshank's sketch for the job is on the back.

117 Hazlitt, Complete Works, XI, pp. 240–1, 'Conversations of James Northcote'. Hazlitt earlier developed this thought more fully in his 'Common Places', 1823, XX, pp. 136–7.

118 *Monthly Magazine*, February 1833, p. 136.

119 *Loyalist's Magazine*, p. 46.

120 *Fraser's Magazine*, August 1833, p. 190.

121 *The Journal of Mrs Arbuthnot, 1820–1832*, ed. Francis Bamford, 1950, p. 39.

122 Ibid., p. 26.

123 Ibid., p. 16.

124 *The Private Letters of Princess Lieven to Prince Metternich, 1820–26*, ed. Peter Quennell, 1948, p. 116.

125 *Loyalist's Magazine*, p. 99.

126 Byron, 'The Irish Avatar', first published 1831.

127 Hazlitt, *Complete Works*, XII, p. 214, 'On the Look of a Gentleman'.

128 Aspinall, *The Correspondence of George Prince of Wales*, 1963–71, VIII, p. 433.

129 *The English Spy*, 1826, p. 33.

130 Collection of Ronald Searle.

131 *Quarterly Review*, December 1854, p. 78.

132 Hazlitt, *Complete Works*, VIII, p. 112.

133 *The Northern Excursion of Geordie*, 1822.

134 'The English-Irish Highlandman', 1822.

135 *Blackwood's Magazine*, July 1823, pp. 21–2.

136 Ibid., p. 22.

137 Knight, *Passages*, II, p. 7.

138 *The English Spy*, 1825, I, p. 187.

139 *Greenwich Hospital*, 1826, pp. 63–4, 115–16.

140 *The English Spy*, I, p. 347.

141 *Blackwood's Magazine*, June 1827, pp. 777, 785.

142 *Monthly Magazine*, February 1833, pp. 142–4.

143 *The Cigar*, I, pp. 7–8.

144 *The Every-Day Book*, 1825, col. 638.

145 *The English Spy*, 1826, II, p. 82.

146 *Portraits of Public Characters*, II, p. 246.

147 *George Cruikshank's Omnibus*, 1842, p. 5.

148 Vizetelly, *Glances Back*, I, p. 105.

APPENDIX & BIBLIOGRAPHY

ISAAC CRUIKSHANK

Baptized Canongate Parish, Edinburgh, 14 October 1764 (but baptisms were often some time after birth).

Married Mary McNaughton, 14 August 1788, St Anne's, Soho (parish records, Westminster Library).

Was living at 1 St Martin's Court, Westminster, in 1789, and 7 St Martin's Court in 1790 (Royal Academy records).

First child, Isaac Robert, baptized St Martin-in-the-Fields 25 October 1789, aged four weeks (Westminster Library).

Living in Duke Street, Bloomsbury, 1792–4 (rate books, Holborn Public Library, give no numbers, but show that the Regent Lion Service Station, Coptic Street, now occupies the site of George's birth).

First appears in rate books for Dorset Street, St Bride's Parish, 1808.

Buried St Bride's Church, 16 April 1811 (records at Guildhall, City of London, give his age as 48, which puts birth date between April 1762 and April 1763).

GEORGE CRUIKSHANK

Born Duke Street (now Coptic Street), 27 September 1792; baptized St George's, Bloomsbury, 6 November 1792 (parish records, Greater London Record Office).

Apparently left 117 Dorset Street in 1819.

Leased 25 Myddelton Terrace, 1824; which was renumbered 22 Amwell Street by 1826 (though he still called it Myddelton Terrace). Moved to 23 Amwell Street, 1834. Nos 22 and 23 were renumbered 69 and 71 Amwell Street in 1936 (rate books, Finsbury Library).

Sister, Margaret Eliza, died August 1825, aged 18.

First wife, Mary Ann, died 28 May 1849, aged 42 (so she was born in the same year as the sister. Did George marry his sister's school friend?).

Married Eliza Widdison of Dalby Terrace, Finsbury, 8 March 1850, and moved to 48 Mornington Place (now 263 Hampstead Road, Camden).

Mother, Mary Cruikshank, died at 48 Mornington Place, August 1853, aged nearly 84.

George Cruikshank died, 263 Hampstead Road, 1 February 1878, aged 85. He is buried in St Paul's Cathedral.

Cruikshank's will revealed that he had maintained a second household not far away at 31 Augustus Street. He left the bulk of his property to Adelaide Archibold of that address, and thereafter to her ten children (the youngest born March 1875); and she also got the 'furniture, books, wines [!] and household effects belonging to me . . . in the said house', so it cannot be thought to have been a case of mere friendship.

BIBLIOGRAPHY

The notes on pages 140–41 provide a wide-ranging guide to material for George Cruikshank's earlier life and times. Some other works are:

Douglas, R. J. H., *The Works of George Cruikshank, Classified and Arranged . . .*, 1903

Feaver, William, and Arts Council of Great Britain, Catalogue of George Cruikshank exhibition, Victoria & Albert Museum, 1974; 85 illustrations, mainly of later work

George, M. Dorothy, *Catalogue of Political and Personal Satires*, vols VI–XI, 1938–1954; details of more than 9,000 caricatures of the period 1792–1832 in British Museum collection. *Hogarth to Cruikshank: Social Change in Graphic Satire*, 1967. *English Political Caricature*, 2 vols, Oxford, 1959

Hancock, Charles, ed., *A Handbook for Posterity: or Recollections of Twiddle Twaddle by George Cruikshank*, 1896; sixty-two illustrations by George Cruikshank, partly autobiographical, but often with shaky or nonsensical explanations

Krumhaar, E. B., *Isaac Cruikshank: A Catalogue Raisonné*, Philadelphia, 1966; not error-free

McLean, Ruari, *George Cruikshank: His Life and Work as a Book Illustrator*, 1948; 54 pages of reproductions

Patten, Robert L., ed., *George Cruikshank: A Revaluation*, Princeton University Library, 1974; mainly on the later years; 44 illustrations

Richardson, Benjamin Ward (George Cruikshank's executor), *Drawings by George Cruikshank, Prepared by Him to Illustrate an Intended Autobiography*, 1895; many of the same drawings as in Hancock, sometimes with even shakier explanations

INDEX

The caricature appearances of a few much-caricatured persons
are specially indicated for easier reference